TO MR AND MRS FERNANDEZ!

THANKS FOR MAKING MY NEW "BABY" READABLE!

ENJOY THE MAGIC BEAUTY OF MARYLAND!

Fishing Boat, Rock Hall, Kent County

MARYLAND A PORTRAIT

Written By
Roger Miller
Anne Heroux-Murphy

Photography By
Roger Miller

Port Herman, Cecil County

Photo of Roger Miller

IMAGE PUBLISHING, LTD.

IMAGE PUBLISHING, LTD.
1411 Hollins Street/Union Square
410-566-1222   Baltimore, Maryland 21223   FAX 410-233-1241

DEDICATION

ADRIENNE MONNINGER-MILLER

I would like to re-dedicate this new Maryland book to my daughter, Adrienne. I am so glad you could be my photo assistant on some of the shooting of this book. I know we both learned a lot from the experience. Cool! Love You!

ROGER MILLER, 5-20-96

SPECIAL THANKS

I would like to thank everyone who had a part in this project. I would especially like to thank the following:

A special thanks to **RUTH AND CHARLES MILLER,** my parents for their assistance, love and courage no matter what.

A special thanks to **MASTER JIM HUMPHRIES** for his assistance and focus.

I would like to thank **GOVERNOR PARRIS GLENDENING** for his invaluable assistance in writing the foreword to "Maryland A Portrait."

A special thanks to **TOM CARTER** of Old Bay Financial for his assistance, friendship, advice and action.

A special thanks to **LYNN MOQUIN, CPA** for her financial advice, friendship and moral support over the last couple of years.

I would like to thank **THE BANK OF GLEN BURNIE** for their belief in my work and the opportunity to continue to create our books.

I would like to thank **JUDY KRUSE** for her patience and diligent assistance with proofreading this book. What's the rule for commas?

I would like to thank **ANNE HEROUX-MURPHY** for putting up with some of the pressure we have dealt with in creating our books.

ROGER MILLER, 5-20-96

CREDITS

Photography by Roger Miller

Design by David Miller

Foreword by Governor Parris Glendening

Writing Text by Roger Miller

Writing Captions by Roger Miller & Anne Heroux-Murphy

Editing by Roger Miller

Photo Typesetting by Delta Graphics & Communications, Inc.

INFORMATION

Library of Congress Catalogue Card Number: 96-94508 (3rd Edition)

First Printing 1986, Second Printing 1988, Third Printing 1990, Fourth Printing 1992, Fifth Printing 1996.

Printed in Hong Kong.

ORDERS

For direct orders please call or write for specific cost and postage and handling to the above address. Discounts available for stores, institutions and corporations, minimum orders required.

STATE HOUSE, ANNAPOLIS - is the oldest state house in the country in continuous operation. The dome at the top reflects the proud tradition of freedom began by the Calverts and it is the largest wooden dome in the United States. At one time the State House was the Capitol of the United States.

FREDERICK COUNTY FARM - The snow comes early in Western Maryland and stays on the ground longer. Farmers in Western Maryland need to watch the weather carefully in both the spring and fall so as not to be suprised by snow.

TABLE OF CONTENTS

FOREWORD - PARRIS GLENDENING, GOVERNOR 6

INTRODUCTION & HISTORY 8

CENTRAL MARYLAND 10

    ANNE ARUNDEL COUNTY 12

    PRINCE GEORGE'S COUNTY 26

    MONTGOMERY COUNTY 32

    HOWARD COUNTY 38

    BALTIMORE COUNTY 44

    BALTIMORE CITY 48

    HARFORD COUNTY 58

EASTERN SHORE 64

    CECIL COUNTY 66

    KENT COUNTY 70

    QUEEN ANNE'S COUNTY 74

    CAROLINE COUNTY 78

    TALBOT COUNTY 82

    DORCHESTER COUNTY 88

    SOMERSET COUNTY 92

    WICOMICO COUNTY 96

    WORCESTER COUNTY 100

SOUTHERN MARYLAND 104

    ST. MARY'S COUNTY 106

    CHARLES COUNTY 112

    CALVERT COUNTY 116

WESTERN MARYLAND 120

    CARROLL COUNTY 122

    FREDERICK COUNTY 126

    WASHINGTON COUNTY 130

    ALLEGANY COUNTY 136

    GARRETT COUNTY 140

ECONOMY - PORT 146

GOVERNOR PARRIS N. GLENDENING - welcomes President Clinton and Vice President Gore to
commemorate Earth Day at the town of Havre De Grace in Harford County.
Governor Glendening meets with a group of police from around the state for a press conference in the
Governor's reception room at the State House.

FOREWORD

By Parris N. Glendening, Governor

Rugged mountains...rolling hills...pastoral countryside...exciting cities...the majestic Chesapeake Bay...graceful tidewater towns...and the Atlantic Ocean. All of this and more can be found in Maryland.

While living, working and raising a family in Maryland, I have always been proud of my State and my fellow citizens. As Governor, my pride has deepened because I have seen the enthusiasm Marylanders have for their homes, their jobs, their communities and their State.

As you look through the beautiful photographs in *Maryland A Portrait*, you will see a kaleidoscope of images of Maryland. The log canoe skimming across the water represents Maryland's rich maritime heritage. The bustling city of Baltimore brings to mind Maryland's strong commitment to its port and expanding biotechnology industry. The images of the State House in Annapolis, the cannons at Antietam National Battlefield and the star-shaped Fort McHenry serve as reminders of the important role Maryland has played in our nation's history. Photographs of NASA's Goddard Space Flight Center and our growing high-technology industry illustrate Maryland's commitment to the future as we prepare for the next century.

If a picture is worth a thousand words, this book demonstrates that Maryland has an impressive story to tell. Maryland's history began long before the first European explorers came to its shores in the 1600's. The Algonquian tribes of the Choptank, Nanticoke, Patuxent, Portabago and Wicomico rivers fished the waters of the Chesapeake Bay, named because of the abundance of shellfish in its waters. This rich natural environment also attracted European settlers to the Chesapeake Bay, and in 1634 English colonists came to Maryland under a land charter granted by King George I of England to the first Lord Baltimore. These early settlers thrived in such a bountiful land.

Today, Maryland remains a great place to live and work. Our State offers an outstanding quality of life for its residents, an exciting and diverse business community, a superior educational system, fine arts and cultural activities, first-class parks and recreational facilities, and an excellent transportation infrastructure.

Maryland's diversity attracts visitors from around the world. When we talk about the number of outstanding attractions the State has to offer, we now say, "Maryland. So many things to do. So close together." That's because you can spend the morning people-watching along the Atlantic Ocean boardwalk in Ocean City, and then travel a mere 30 miles to enjoy a crab feast on a deck overlooking the Chesapeake Bay. You can visit Baltimore's museums, shops and famous Inner Harbor, or take a short drive to Annapolis and explore the cobblestone streets of Maryland's State capital or visit the U.S. Naval Academy. In Western Maryland you can ski the slopes in winter or try your hand at fly fishing on a quiet mountain stream or enjoy boating on Deep Creek Lake during the spring and summer months.

This is an exciting time in Maryland. Emerging technologies, enhanced educational programs and a business-friendly attitude demonstrate Maryland's commitment to excellence. In the fields of bio-technology and medical research, Maryland is rapidly becoming an international center, demonstrated by the world-renowned Johns Hopkins and the Columbus Center, a marine biology research center in Baltimore.

Maryland's transportation system is one of the best in the world. The Port of Baltimore has brought Maryland world-wide attention for its highly efficient cargo handling. And, Baltimore/Washington International (BWI) Airport, centrally located between two cities, is one of the fastest growing airports in the region.

This book gives the reader an insight into the beauty, diversity and excitement that is Maryland. Roger, through the lens of his camera, has brought to life the many facets of our State in this very special book. The beauty of the landscape...the vibrancy of the cities...the pride of its citizens have all been captured in a moment in time, in images that entice us to appreciate the richness that is Maryland.

Parris N. Glendening

GREEN RIDGE STATE PARK, ALLEGANY COUNTY - Maryland is a relatively small state but it is big in the variety of environments it has. From Atlantic Coast beaches, to the marshes of the Chesapeake Bay, to the rolling grasslands of Central Maryland to these awesome mountainous views in Western Maryland, it seems as if the state has an area to suit anyone.

INTRODUCTION & HISTORY

Maryland is the home of the black-eyed Susan, the Chesapeake Bay, the Orioles, the blue crab, and the Preakness. "Oh say can you see ..." was written by Francis Scott Key at Ft. McHenry in Maryland. The ground of Maryland was broken and became home to the first "National" road and the first railroad in the country. Along the Potomac River, Washington and L'Enfant laid plans for the nation's capital and this tract of Maryland is now home to Washington, D.C. The richness and diversity of Maryland has cultivated and is the home to many firsts, many great men and women, much history, and if you listen very quietly, you can hear the stirring of the seeds of even greater things to come.

Located in the heart of the eastern seaboard nestled just below the Mason-Dixon line, Maryland is the nation's ninth smallest state with 9,837 square miles. Maryland has a population of about five million which makes it both in size and population inauspicious.

Diversity and abundance defines Maryland's glory. It is known justly as "America in Miniature" because you can find landscapes to satisfy almost anyone. Maryland is located on a richly forested alluvial plane lying between the Appalachian Mountains and the Atlantic Ocean. The climate of Maryland is for the most part warm and temperate. The western part of the state has more severe winter weather.

The history of Maryland is long and distinguished. Before the European colonization of Maryland which began in the early 1600's, the Native Americans resided here for thousands of years. In 1607, Captain John Smith first sailed and explored the area of the Potomac and Patuxent Rivers. It was not until 1632 that the plans for the colonization of Maryland were formulated by Leonard, Philip, and Cecelius Calvert. Their late father George Calvert, the first Lord of Baltimore, had been granted the colony by the English Crown. The colonization of Maryland for the Calverts was not simply for the accumulation of wealth, but to establish a society founded on religious freedom. The persecution they had endured in Europe would be the catalyst for religious freedom in Maryland.

The first settlers landed on St. Clement's Island on March 25, 1634. After preliminary exploration they founded their first town a little south in St. Mary's City. They were encouraged to plant both substance crops as well as revenue crops such as tobacco. Within the first year the colonists had founded a legislative assembly. The Toleration Act of 1649 granted the freedom of religion throughout Maryland-the realization of George Calvert's original dream. The difficulties faced by the early colony were many. It was not until 1689 that political stability could be found in Maryland. Growth, however had proceeded steadily from the beginning. Settlements were developed to the north and east of St. Mary's County. Kent County was founded in 1642, Anne Arundel County in 1650, Charles County in 1658 and Calvert County in 1654. The city of Annapolis in Anne Arundel County became the new State Capital in 1695. By the end of the 1600's the map of Maryland had been carefully divided.

The early 1700's found steady growth in commerce and a steady increase in the population. In 1729, Baltimore was founded as a commercial center. Maryland's economy was almost wholly agricultural at that time and the chief crop was tobacco. By the time of the American Revolution there were approximately 250,000 colonists in Maryland. In the early 1700's there was also the beginning of settlements to the west. Frederick was established by 1745. Hagerstown was chartered in 1752, and a fort stood in Cumberland by 1755.

The spirit of freedom and revolution had been evolving throughout the 1700's. The "Old Line State" sent five representatives to the Continental Congress and assumed a leadership role from the beginning in the Revolutionary War. For a time Baltimore was the seat of the Congress and Maryland troops participated in nearly every major military campaign. At the close of the War, Annapolis became the temporary capital of the newly founded country.

Between the Revolutionary War and The War of 1812 there was enormous economic growth in Maryland. With peace there was time for the development of cultural and educational institutions. Washington College in Chestertown was founded in 1782, the first college established in the United States. St. John's College was founded in 1784, and in 1785 the University of Maryland was established.

The War of 1812 again put Maryland into political and economic turmoil. The second war with Great Britain was fought over commercial freedom, an issue important to Maryland. Maryland would become the center of the fighting in this war with Britain. In 1813 the British attacked and burned Washington, sending the congress and most of the government fleeing into the Maryland countryside. In 1814 the British returned under the command of Admiral Cockburn and landed troops in North Point just outside of Baltimore. All the while British battleships proceeded with a bombardment of Ft. McHenry at the entrance of the Baltimore Harbor. Baltimore and the fort endured a siege throughout the 13th of September 1814. Francis Scott Key depicted this noble battle in what is now our national anthem. Admiral Cockburn and the British departed and a peace treaty was signed before the end of the year.

Growth began again at the end of the war. This time it was directed toward the western part of the state. By 1815, Baltimore was the third largest port in America. The Chesapeake and Ohio Canal was completed from Georgetown to Cumberland by 1830. Charles Carroll of Carrollton laid the cornerstone of the Baltimore and Ohio Railroad on July 4, 1828 and this marked what was notably the most important commercial event of the century.

The peace and prosperity that had taken hold after the War of 1812 began to deteriorate in the late 1850's. The controversy over slavery divided Maryland severely. The talk and feelings toward secession were very strong, but the Federal Capital lay within her borders. Maryland took a prudent course and remained Union. Maryland would again see blood spilled on her soil, in April of 1861 a riot in Baltimore resulted in the first bloodshed of the Civil War. In September of 1863 the rural calm of the town of Sharpsburg was shattered by the Battle of Antietam.

At the end of the Civil War, much of the state returned to life as it had been. For Baltimore the post-Civil War years were a period of unprecedented economic growth. Baltimoreans grew rich with exports of grain, cattle and tobacco as well as the imports of coffee, iron ore, and chemicals. This new wealth found it's way back into the community. This was an era of great philanthropy creating many new institutions such as the Peabody Institute in 1866, the Johns Hopkins University in 1876 and the Enoch Pratt Free Library in 1882.

Maryland's prominence in national affairs has continued to this day. In the pages to follow we will explore in words and pictures most of Maryland's monuments, her industries, and her institutions. We will also explore, county by county, her natural beauty which after 350 years of development remains exciting, fresh, and wondrous.

FULL MOON, MONTPELIER MANSION - The rolling hills of Central Maryland seem calm as the moon rises over the trees at Montpelier Mansion. This is a quiet reprieve from the fast pace of life in this Central Maryland business corridor, between Baltimore and Washington, D.C.

CENTRAL MARYLAND

Central Maryland stretches through the middle of the state from Pennsylvania to Virginia. It is made up of gentle rolling hills which lie between the mountains to the west and the Chesapeake Bay. This area is part of the east coast megalopolis. Most of Maryland's population live and work in this region. The majority of commerce and business occurs in this area. Maryland's capital and largest cities are located here.

The area is comprised of six counties and the city of Baltimore. This region is often called the "corridor counties", which refers to the interstate highway systems running through the area. The most notable of these roadways is I-95. As intense and crowded as this area is, fifteen minutes outside of Baltimore or Washington you will find farms, horses, waterfalls, and forests. Actually this area is rich with some of the finest farms and scenery in the state. Most of this natural beauty is foreshadowed by the cosmopolitan urban centers which "scream" for attention.

Anne Arundel County is the most logical place to begin exploring Central Maryland. It is home of the state capital in Annapolis. Anne Arundel County is rather large and stretches from Baltimore City in the north to Calvert County in the south. The Bay, its eastern border, is broken by numerous rivers while in the west there is only the Patuxent River.

Annapolis sits at the convergence of the Severn River and the Chesapeake Bay on three peninsulas. It has over 16 miles of shoreline. Even though Annapolis is the political center of the state the city is also one of the historic gems of Maryland. Annapolis is one of the most pristine kept Colonial cities in America. It is filled with important historical sites such as the Chase-Lloyd House, the William Paca House, and the Hammond-Harwood House. At the top of the hill in Annapolis is the State House and across the street is Government House where the Governor of Maryland resides. Annapolis with Spa Creek, the South River and the Severn River all meeting as they flow into the Chesapeake Bay is also one of the sailing capitals of the world. In 1845 Annapolis became the home of the United States Naval Academy. Across the Severn River and slightly north is the William Preston Lane Memorial Bridge. It is known to everyone in Maryland as the Chesapeake Bay Bridge and ties Central Maryland with the Eastern Shore.

Prince George's County is just across the Patuxent River to the west of Anne Arundel County. It is a very long county and stretches from Howard County in the north to Charles County in the south. The southeastern part of the county is similar to Southern Maryland with tobacco barns and scenic fields. The northern part of the county is caught up in the whirling world of Washington. College Park, in the north, is the flagship of the University of Maryland and the location of a new structure to house much of the collection of the National Archives. The NASA Goddard Space Flight Center is located a little to the east. Montpelier Mansion is just to the north. Slightly south is Andrews Air Force Base. Established in 1942 by president Roosevelt, Andrews is now the gateway to the nation.

Montgomery County is located to the northwest of Washington. The southeastern part is caught up amidst the politics and business of the nation's capital. The northwestern part of the county is quiet and resembles Western Maryland rather than Washington. There are so many "National Institutes" from Washington to Rockville that it would be difficult to list them all. The National Institutes of Health (NIH) and the National Medical Library are located in Bethesda. The Mormon Temple dramatically rises up from the capital beltway as if it is from another place and time. The C&O Canal runs from Georgetown all along the Potomac River. Numerous sites along the canal have been restored. The most dramatic of these is at Great Falls, where the Potomac River turns into raging white water rapids.

Howard County is located to the northeast of Montgomery County. Howard County, because of its' location , has become a sort of "bedroom" community for both Baltimore and Washington. The city of Columbia in the middle of the east side of the county is a first in Maryland. It is a new totally planned city which only opened in 1967. It has grown to encompass over half the population of Howard County. Ellicott City to the east on the other hand has existed since 1772. It began as a gristmill company town. Today Ellicott City is full of upscale shops and restaurants. The west part of the county is quieter; there are fewer houses and more farms.

Baltimore County stretches from Pennsylvania in the north to Anne Arundel County in the south. Baltimore County completely surrounds Baltimore City and is part of the richness of Maryland's largest cosmopolitan center. Towson, directly north of Baltimore is a commercial hub in its' own right. Towson is less dense and more green than Baltimore. The Hampton Mansion, located in Towson, is a 40 room Georgian mansion that was once the center of a huge estate. North of Towson there is fox hunting, horse racing, wondrous farms, and the Jericho Covered Bridge. The eastern part of the county offers boating and marinas along the Back, Middle, and Gunpowder Rivers and the Chesapeake Bay.

Baltimore City is situated at the bottom center of Baltimore County. In the last 20 years it blossomed from a deteriorated rust belt city into a tourist mecca. Even the most die hard skeptics who said they would never venture downtown have been seen strolling along the Inner Harbor. The National Aquarium, The Baltimore Museum of Art, The Peabody Conservatory of Music, The Walters Art Gallery, The Meyerhoff Symphony Hall, The Washington Monument, and Ft. McHenry are just a few of the sites to be enjoyed in the largest city in Maryland.

Harford County is located directly to the northeast of Baltimore City . It is nestled between Pennsylvania, the Susquehannah River and the Chesapeake Bay. The largest employer is the Aberdeen Proving Grounds, where Army weapons are tested. A huge ordinance museum is open to the public in Aberdeen. Ladew Topiary Gardens in the northern part of the county is a world class garden. The historic Liriodendron Mansion was the Bel Air home of the "Teddy Roosevelt like" Doctor Kelly, one of the founding fathers of Johns Hopkins Hospital. In Havre de Grace is the Concord Point Lighthouse and one of the largest decoy museums in the state. Harford County is full of small creeks and horse farms where you can find fox hunts in the fall. Polo is also played at Ladew Gardens in the fall. In the north along the Susquehanna and the Bay are numerous marinas and sailing.

Central Maryland is the populated business center of the state but it is rich in scenic and historic beauty. A visit to it's urban centers will enrich you as will a tour of its countryside.

ANNE ARUNDEL COUNTY

Sitting directly south of Baltimore City and running along the edge of the Chesapeake Bay, is Anne Arundel County. It is here that Maryland's capital of Annapolis is located.

ANNAPOLIS, AERIAL VIEW - At the center of this aerial view of Annapolis is the State House on State Circle. To the far left is the Severn River along it's banks is the Naval Academy. Spa Creek flows into the Severn River and is to the south and on the right side of the photo.

MARYLAND STATE HOUSE, ANNAPOLIS - Built on the highest point of land it is the visual focal point of Annapolis. The Maryland State House veritably and symbolically governs the state capital. Like spokes, the streets seem to diverge from the State House in the center, forming a city in the shape of a wheel.

St. John's College

Chase-Lloyd House

Hammond-Harwood House

Governor's Mansion

GOVERNOR'S MANSION, ANNAPOLIS - This beautiful Victorian mansion is the Governor's residence.
ST. JOHN'S COLLEGE - founded as King William's School in 1696 it is one of America's first public educational institutions. **CHASE-LLOYD MANSION** - Construction of this Georgian mansion was originated in 1769 by Samuel Chase, a signer of The Declaration of Independence. **HAMMOND-HARWOOD HOUSE** - This Georgian style house is one of the most impressive examples of late Colonial architecture in America.

State House - Senate Chambers

MARYLAND STATE HOUSE, ANNAPOLIS - The Maryland State House contains both the Senate and the House of Delegates chambers where Maryland's legislature meets for three months out of each year. The Maryland State House also served as the Capitol of the United States from November 1783 to August 1784.

PACA HOUSE & GARDENS, ANNAPOLIS - This Georgian Mansion was constructed between 1763 and 1765 by William Paca. He was a signer of The Declaration of Independence and later became Governor of Maryland. A Chinese Trellis Bridge can be found in this two acre, 18th century garden as well as a domed pavilion and a fish shaped pond.

ANNAPOLIS HARBOR - It was almost as if God created Annapolis to be a sailing town. There are 16 miles of protected waterfront in and around Annapolis. The rivers and marinas of Annapolis have more sailboats than almost any other place on the east coast.

SAILING, ANNAPOLIS - A view from the top of the mast on *Airwaves*, an asset of the Naval Academy Sailing Team, gives an exciting vista of the sailing experience in Annapolis. Almost any day of the year you can see these Naval Academy sailboats gliding along the Severn River and into the Chesapeake Bay.

U.S. NAVAL ACADEMY SAILING TEAM - The Naval Academy has a fleet of sailboats in its'
Santee Basin right on the Severn River. Midshipmen learn to sail and navigate with sextants as well as
satellites while on board the sailboats.

Bancroft Hall Lobby

Naval Chapel, Interior

BANCROFT HALL - is named after the founder of the Naval Academy, Secretary of the Navy, George Bancroft. It is the largest dormitory in the world, housing all 4,000 midshipmen. **MEMORIAL HALL** - at the entrance of Bancroft Hall, is full of historic Naval memorabilia. **THE NAVAL ACADEMY CHAPEL** - is the tallest building at the academy. The resting place for John Paul Jones is an architectural wonder with stained glass windows by Louis Comfort Tiffany.

U.S. NAVAL ACADEMY, NOON FORMATION - The Midshipmen line up before noon meal in Tecumseh Court in front of Bancroft Hall. Bancroft Hall is the largest dormitory in the world. Over one million visitors come to the Naval Academy each year, most of them trying to observe noon meal formation if the weather permits.

21

Propulsion Lab

Hull Test Lab

U.S. NAVAL ACADEMY, CLASSES - Besides the parades and the fancy uniforms, the Naval Academy is four years of intense academic growth. There are 600 members of the faculty which are almost equally mixed between civilian and military personnel. Not seen by many visitors, their labs and facilities are some of the finest in the world. Graduates receive a Bachelor of Science degree even if they major in the humanities.

U.S. NAVAL ACADEMY, HERNDON MONUMENT - The Herndon Monument, at the end of each year, becomes a right of passage for the freshmen class called "Plebes." After this first year of trials the obelisk is the final challenge to overcome. With team work the class scales the monument which is greased with 200 pounds of lard. At the top is a taped down plebe hat (dixie cup) which is to be replaced with an upper classman's hat. The plebe that replaces the hat is said to become the first Admiral of the class.

Colors Parade

Blue Angels Fly Over

Graduates

Colors Parade

U.S. NAVAL ACADEMY, GRADUATION - After four years of intense academic and military training,
midshipmen celebrate graduation with a traditional week of activities and ceremonies.
Midshipmen are all full time military, after graduation they are required to serve five years in
either the Navy or the Marine Corps.

U.S. NAVAL ACADEMY, GRADUATION - The hat toss marks the graduation for these midshipmen. The hat toss is symbolic of their commissioning as ensigns in the Navy or 2nd lieutenants in the Marine Corps. They no longer need their midshipmen hats, after the hat toss they don their new hats as officers.

University of Maryland, College Park

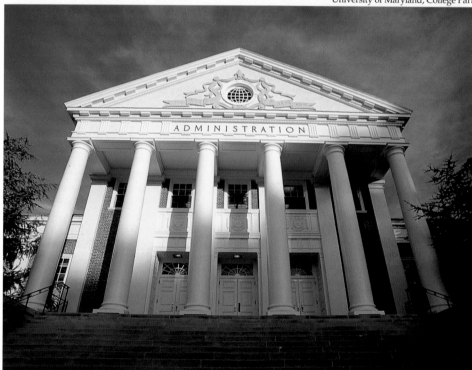

Silver Spring

University of Maryland, College Park

PRINCE GEORGE'S COUNTY

Prince George's County is a rather large county located in the southern part of Central Maryland. It is bordered by the Patuxent River on the east and Washington, D.C. on the south and west.

THE UNIVERSITY OF MARYLAND, COLLEGE PARK - The University of Maryland, College Park is the "flagship" to one of the first university systems in the nation. **SILVER SPRING** - The most urban area in Prince George's County, Silver Spring is where the political, economic, and cultural influences of Washington are the most evident.

CALVERT MANSION - Built by Belgian nobility this replica of an 18th century Belgian mansion was the home of Charles Benedict Calvert. Once the property of a "founding father" it is now a newly restored site and a rich contribution of Prince George's County to Maryland's historical preservation.

Blue Angels, Andrews A.F.B.

NASA Goddard Space Center

Blue Angels, Andrews A.F.B.

NASA Goddard Space Center

BLUE ANGELS - The Blue Angels sometimes perform their air show at Andrews Air Force Base located in Prince George's County. Now flying in the sleek McDonald Douglas F/A-18 Hornets, the Blue Angels celebrated their 50th anniversary in 1996. **NASA GODDARD SPACE CENTER** - The hub for tracking all of NASA's world space flight activities is located at the NASA Goddard Space Center in Prince George's County. The museum is open to the public for tours.

President Clinton at Andrews Air Force Base

ANDREWS AIR FORCE BASE - Originally built as an Army air field in 1942 by President Roosevelt, Andrews Air Force Base is now the home to the president's private plane, Air Force One. Andrews is where most visiting dignitaries are welcomed by the president making Prince George's County and Maryland the "gateway" to the country.

UPPER MARLBORO - About an hour from Silver Spring, as you enter the southeastern area of Prince George's County, the urban fades into the rural. Large fields, farms and tobacco barns dot the landscape, evidence of the Colonial plantations which once flourished there and the traditions they passed on.

MONTPELIER MANSION - Located in northern Prince George's County the historic Montpelier Mansion was built in the 1770's by Major Thomas Snowden. It has been preserved by the state due to its architectural beauty and historic value. A Cultural Arts Center has been built to accompany the mansion and grounds.

Bethesda/I-270 Corridor

Capitol Building - Washington, D.C.

MONTGOMERY COUNTY

Montgomery County is the transition between the urban northeastern area of Washington and the mountainous countryside of Frederick County. One of the most affluent counties in the state and nation it has the highest per capita income in Maryland.

BETHESDA - The beginning of the I-270 corridor, Bethesda is known for its impressive architecture. Bethesda's focus on commercial activity is influenced by its proximity to Washington, D.C.

MORMON TEMPLE - Considered by many as the "emerald city" of Montgomery County, the Mormon Temple is a stirring and majestic presence on the Washington beltway. Its exhibits and beautiful gardens are open to the public. The temple and its grounds are traditionally decorated with over 400,000 lights for the Christmas season.

Garrett Park

Clara Barton House

Glen Echo Park/Carousel

Clara Barton House

GARRETT PARK - Circa 1898 the beautiful area of Garrett Park is a registered historic district within Montgomery County, containing an arboretum and numerous stunning homes. **GLEN ECHO PARK** - Opened as a recreational park in 1891, Glen Echo Park is home to a beautifully hand carved Dentzel carousel from 1921. The park, its amusements, ballroom for dances, children's theater, and art gallery are all open to the public. **CLARA BARTON HOUSE** - This historical site dating from 1891 was the home to the founder of the American Red Cross. At one time it served as both a headquarters and a warehouse for the Red Cross and is now open for guided tours.

National Institutes of Health

Bethesda Naval Hospital

NIH - NATIONAL INSTITUTES OF HEALTH - Located along Montgomery County's I-270 corridor, the National Institutes of Health is the federal bureau entrusted with health research. It is open to the public for tours. **BETHESDA NAVAL HOSPITAL** - This hospital is one of the many examples of Washington, D.C.'s influence in Montgomery County.

C&O Canal at Great Falls

POTOMAC RIVER, GREAT FALLS - Proof of Montgomery County's diversity is the Great Falls.
The falls rush with white water inviting anyone challenged by kayaking. The area is a favorite spot for
hiking, fishing, picnics, biking, and jogging. It is conveniently located one half hour from Bethesda and the
I-270 corridor.

POTOMAC RIVER, GREAT FALLS & C&O CANAL - There are many areas surrounding the I-270 corridor in Montgomery County that are quite rural and rich with natural beauty. To the southeast there are amazing vistas along the Potomac river creating a perfect place for hiking and picnicking. The tow-path for the C&O Canal is a favorite spot for hikers. The C&O Canal National Historic Park offers mule pulled barge rides along parts of the Potomac River. Foot bridges in the park afford hikers fantastic views of Great Falls.

HOWARD COUNTY

Howard County lies southwest of Baltimore City in Central Maryland. It is located between Baltimore and Washington and occupies a large stretch of Interstate 95.

COLUMBIA - Intentionally constructed by Maryland's acclaimed developer, James Rouse, the town of Columbia is one of the first pre-planned cities in the U.S. Over the years it has grown to accommodate one half the population and businesses of Howard County.

COLUMBIA - Purposely landscaped and designed for convenience, The Columbia Town Center is the shopping and recreation area completely encircled by residential Columbia. Like everything in Columbia the lake is next to the town center.

ELLICOTT CITY - Ellicott City hums with music and visitors, especially on the weekends. Wonderful specialty shops, antique shops and restaurants line the small old fashioned streets. Once a 17th century grist mill town on the Patapsco River its stone structures have become a happy hunting ground for anyone in search of curiosities and antiques. It is also home to a historic railroad museum and is only a short drive from Baltimore.

BELMONT - Belmont has welcomed distinguished visitors with warmth and grace since 1738, when Caleb Dorsey built the splendid Georgian mansion as the manor house for one of Maryland's great estates. Belmont Manor House and Meeting Facility continues to offer a gracious atmosphere and private working environment to all groups concerned with the pursuit and sharing of knowledge. When you travel the tree-lined lane through the gates of Belmont, it becomes your private meeting place.

ELKRIDGE FURNACE INN - The Elkridge Furnace Inn is now a restaurant but it once functioned as a Colonial seaport tavern. An iron smelting furnace was built near the tavern by Caleb Dorsey. Due to its rich historic background the inn was saved, before demolition, by concerned citizens in the 1980's. It is now leased to The Wecker's, Inc., Gourmet Caterers and is a perfect place to celebrate a wedding, hold a group function or enjoy an intimate meal.

WESTERN HOWARD COUNTY - Western Howard County unlike the populated eastern part has less houses and more farms, less people and more cows, and less lawns and more alfalfa fields. There is a lot of development between the farms but much of this area remains as it was 100 years ago.

BALTIMORE COUNTY

Baltimore County is a large county extending from Pennsylvania all the way to the Chesapeake Bay.
Baltimore County completely surrounds Baltimore City.

HAMPTON MANSION - Snow covers the grounds of the Hampton Mansion which was once
the center of a huge estate stretching 20 miles both east and west, and almost all the way north to
Pennsylvania. The estate now has 26 buildings and is continually being restored.
The mansion and the grounds are open for tours.

TOWSON - Just north of Baltimore City, Towson has become a major commercial center in
its own right. The aerial view above is looking northeast across Sheppard Pratt Hospital Center
towards the heart of Towson.

Hunt Cup

Pretty Boy Reservoir

Hunt Cup

Boordy Vineyards

HUNT CUP - One of the most prestigious and toughest horse races in the county is the Hunt Cup which takes place every year at the end of April. **LOCH RAVEN AND PRETTY BOY RESERVOIRS** - Just north of Towson are a source of drinking water and a favorite recreational area. Just to the east of Towson **BOORDY VINEYARD** - produces wines that are both locally and internationally recognized.

Jericho Covered Bridge

JERICHO COVERED BRIDGE - Reflecting the rural charm of Baltimore County, the Jericho Covered
Bridge (circa 1864) is still in use in Kingsville. This is a fine example of the rustic charm you can still find in
Baltimore County only forty minutes from the city.

BALTIMORE CITY

Baltimore is the largest city in the state of Maryland. It is the center of most commerce and culture, and has become a important tourist attraction in the last couple of years.

BALTIMORE INNER HARBOR - Baltimore's Inner Harbor is the centerpiece of restoration in Baltimore City. The plans for this restoration originated 30 years ago with Mayor Schaefer and James Rouse.

BALTIMORE INNER HARBOR - A balloon glow at the Inner Harbor celebrates the glory of the city. Restaurants, shops, and attractions line the walkways which wind seven and a half miles through the Inner Harbor. Clean, well lit and fun, the Inner Harbor attracts millions of tourists each year.

Oriole Park

Pimlico

ORIOLE PARK AT CAMDEN YARDS - Baltimore has a long and rich tradition with sports teams. The new stadium at the Inner Harbor is home to the Baltimore Orioles. **THE PREAKNESS AT PIMLICO** - Each year in May the Preakness Stakes are run in Baltimore. The second jewel of the Triple Crown, this race is recognized world wide.

CLARION HOTEL - This stunning view of Mt. Vernon and the Washington Monument is from the George Washington Club high atop the Clarion Hotel. Located in this historic and culturally rich neighborhood just north of the Inner Harbor, the Clarion offers a sophisticated option for both weekend excursions or week-long conferences. Reviewed as "one of the best places to stay in the world" *Conde' Nast Traveler*, 1996, the Clarion offers 103 tastefully appointed guest rooms complete with period furnishings and marbled baths. The George Washington Club is available for receptions and truly monumental affairs.

Peabody Conservatory & Library

Walters Art Gallery

WALTERS ART GALLERY - A world renowned collection of European art is in the original galleries of the Walters. The centerpiece of which is the Italianate courtyard above. The Hackerman House is the new addition and has an important collection of Asian art. **THE PEABODY LIBRARY** - is part of the Peabody Conservatory of Music. The library is worth seeing for its own architectural value.

FT. McHENRY - Ft. McHenry is the site where in 1814 the Americans held back a British attack on Baltimore. Francis Scott Key wrote the "Star Spangled Banner", our national anthem, as a result of this bombardment.

Harbor Court Library

Brighton's Restaurant

Hampton's Restaurant

Lobby Staircase

HARBOR COURT HOTEL - Harbor Court Hotel, overlooking the dazzling Inner Harbor, presides at the summit of the World's foremost purveyors of hospitality. Beyond the sweeping staircase, Hampton's the nation's #2 restaurant as judged by. *Conde' Nast Traveler*, lures diners to experience the ultimate food and wine extravaganza. Next door, Brightons serves breakfast, lunch, dinner, and afternoon tea in an atmosphere of country elegance. From fine dining to fine art and literature, this elegant establishment draws raves from all over the globe.

HYATT REGENCY HOTEL - Centrally located on the Inner Harbor, the Hyatt Regency is Baltimore's foremost hotel since it's opening. Connected by skywalk to the Convention Center, Harborplace, and within walking distance to all major attractions, Hyatt offers it's visitors a wide array of amenities. This 14 story ultra modern glass and steel structure has a six story atrium lobby, 486 guest rooms, 25 suites and a rooftop restaurant and lounge which boasts a spectacular view of the harbor.

Gypsy's Cafe - Union Square

Fells Point

GYPSY'S CAFE -exemplifies Baltimore's neighborhood charm with it's warm service, savory cuisine and eclectic atmosphere. Located in historic Union Square next to the Hollins Market, it has become known for it's exhibits of local art. **FELLS POINT** - From the rooftop of the familiar Admiral Fell Inn, looking east at the Inner Harbor, one can appreciate the charm of Baltimore's neighborhoods.

Charles Village

Union Square

CHARLES VILLAGE - Baltimore is renowned as much for the Inner Harbor as for its neighborhood charm. Charles Village is just north of Mt. Vernon, and is home to Johns Hopkins University.
UNION SQUARE - is located in West Baltimore. This historic old neighborhood was once the home of H.L.Mencken, who's house has been restored and is open for tours.

HARFORD COUNTY

The most northern of the Central Maryland counties, Harford County is abundant with beautiful scenic farms, recreation sites and historic monuments.

FOX HUNT - The Elkridge Harford Hunt Club has access to thousands of acres of fertile farm land to conduct their fox hunts. They hunt throughout the fall season.

GUNPOWDER FALLS - is one of many streams and creeks which run through Harford County. Bel Air is the largest town in Harford County. There has been much development in the county in the last couple of years but most of the area is still mostly wooded and wonderful.

Liriodendron Mansion

Polo Games at Ladew Gardens

Liriodendron Mansion

Jousting

LIRIODENDRON MANSION - Located in Bel Air, Liriodendron is the house of Dr. Kelly, one of the founding fathers of Johns Hopkins Hospital. Liriodendron is the name of the Tulip trees that surround the house. **POLO** - is played throughout the fall at Ladew Topiary Gardens. **JOUSTING** - is the state sport and can be seen throughout Harford County.

LADEW TOPIARY GARDENS - is a wonderfully restored house and gardens of the late Harvey Ladew.
His unique taste can be seen throughout the house with plum colored bathrooms and bedrooms.
The gardens are equally unique and stunning with a life size fox hunt in topiary forms, a Japanese garden,
and other numerous gardens.

Concord Point Lighthouse

CONCORD POINT LIGHTHOUSE - in Havre de Grace, is on the Susquehanna River and marks the site of a battle in the Revolutionary War. The Concord Point Lighthouse (circa 1827) is one of the oldest continuous operating lighthouses in the United States. The lighthouse has been restored and is open on weekends from April to October.

HAVRE DE GRACE - is located on the Susquehanna River as it flows into the Chesapeake Bay.
The skipjack race is part of the decoy museum's annual festival in the spring. Havre de Grace is a quiet
waterfront town full of restored houses, B&B's and shops. There are numerous new developments and
marinas in Havre de Grace but the town remains the quiet historic gem it has always been.

A small creek, Kent Island, Queen Anne's County

This photo reflects the Eastern Shore almost perfectly. Most of the land is low and flat and horizons seem to go on forever. The entire area is a large flood plain or marsh land. The land is laced with rivers, creeks, and streams very slowly working their way to the Chesapeake Bay.

EASTERN SHORE

Maryland's Eastern Shore is made up of nine counties on the Delmarva Peninsula. The Eastern Shore is unique in the character, beauty and richness of its landscape and its residents. Residents of the Eastern Shore think of themselves first as residents of the Shore and second as Marylanders. There is an old joke about a woman who died at the age of 83 in a remote Eastern Shore town. Her parents had brought her to that town from Baltimore when she was still in diapers. "She was O.K.", commented a neighbor at her burial, "for a foreigner". This attitude does not in any way affect their hospitality. They welcome guests with sunshine, water, open arms, and big plates of steamed crabs or fried chicken.

The Delmarva Peninsula is a vast flood plain and wetlands; it is low, flat and variegated with rivers, streams, and creeks. In fact, to understand the area you need to examine both the land and the water. Water to the Eastern Shore is as important as the land. The top two thirds of the peninsula are divided somewhat equally between Maryland on the west and Delaware on the east. The bottom third is occupied completely by Maryland except for a long sliver at the bottom which belongs to Virginia.

Maryland's portion of the peninsula can be divided into three overlapping regions. The lower shore is a vacation mecca for hundreds of thousands of tourists. The middle shore with towns such as Easton and St. Michaels capture the historical and cultural limelight. The upper shore from the Bay Bridge to the Mason-Dixon line is rich with placid farms and quiet historic towns.

Cecil County is at the very top of the upper shore. In a sense, western Cecil County is part of Central Maryland since both I-95 and Route 40 run through the county. The county is mostly rural and prides itself on remaining separate from urban business centers of Central Maryland. Two covered bridges are located in the northern most part of the county. Elk Neck State Park and the Turkey Point Lighthouse are located on the large peninsula jutting into the Bay. In Chesapeake City you can lounge in the numerous B&B's or restaurants and watch the ships along the C&D Canal.

Kent County is between the Sassafras and the Chester Rivers south of Cecil County. Chestertown on the Chester River is a hidden historic gem. The town is full of Georgian and Federal mansions some of which are romantic B&B's. Washington College, the first college in the U.S., is also located there. The farms and scenery of the surrounding countryside are breathtaking. Rock Hall is one of many fishing and boating towns along the Chesapeake Bay. At the southern tip of the county is Eastern Neck Island National Wildlife Refuge.

Queen Anne's County is located below the Chester River south of Kent County. The region north of Route 50 has some of the most productive and picturesque farms in the state. This area is more upper bay than middle bay. Jutting west, out from the bottom of the county, is a large "T" shaped island known as Kent Island. It is at Kent Island where traffic heading east, from Anne Arundel County, first arrives. Routes 301 and 50 cross the county east from the Bay Bridge and is the beginning of the middle shore and the "asphalt ribbon" to Ocean City. Most people, in a rush to reach the ocean, miss the delights of the real Eastern Shore that begin about 50 feet on either side of the road.

The only county which is land locked on the Eastern Shore is Caroline. The county is quiet and rural. The largest city is Denton. The Denton courthouse is in the center of the town and is surrounded by many stunning Georgian and Victorian homes. The Choptank River meanders through Denton and most of the County. Martinack State Park is located on the Choptank River just outside of Denton. Tuckahoe State Park is just to the west on Tuckahoe Creek which flows into the Choptank. Caroline County is popular for its fishing in the spring and summer as well as hunting in the fall and winter.

Talbot County is truly variegated with rivers, creeks and inlets. It is the unofficial center of "Eastern Shore Class". It is hard to imagine that two blocks from Route 50 in Easton there are quiet streets, Victorian buildings, decoy and antique shops. In St. Michaels is the Chesapeake Bay Maritime Museum, a stunning collection of the boats and ships which are part of the area's history. Across the Trent Avon River is the town of Oxford and further on the peninsula is Tilghman Island. The only attraction in Talbot County that is not on the water is the Wye Oak in the northern part of the county.

The lower shore begins in Dorchester County. Most of the county is quiet, hidden and sophisticated. Like Talbot County it is defined by water. You will find the Choptank to the north, the Bay to the east and Nanticoke to the south. Cambridge is the largest town and the center for most of the areas culture and history. Annie Oakley's house, as well as numerous other Georgian, Colonial, and Victorian mansions are popular sites for visitors. The surrounding countryside is alive with beauty at every turn.

Wicomico County is a "hub" county. It touches Dorchester on the west, Somerset in the south, and Worcester to the southeast. At the center of the county is Salisbury, the largest city on the Eastern Shore. The Wicomico River flows from the center of Salisbury into the Bay. Actually Wicomico is full of lyrical scenic landscapes and numerous historic sites. Salisbury has a delightful zoo, Salisbury State University and Newtown. The Newtown area is full of beautiful Victorian and Georgian mansions including the historic Poplar Hill Mansion.

Somerset County occupies the southwest corner of the lower shore. Off of the beaten path, it is tranquil and sophisticated. Princess Anne is the largest town with Teakle Mansion, circa 1802 as it's centerpiece. To the west of Princess Anne is Deal Island, a quiet and quaint fishing village. Crisfield, to the south, is a bit more crowded but only slightly. If there is a town which is the fishing and seafood capital of the region it is Crisfield.

Worcester County , to most, is the Atlantic barrier island which is home to Ocean City. When most Baltimoreans talk of "downtheocean hon" it is Ocean City they mean. This is a year round resort with golf courses, condominiums and beach houses. Assateague Island is a larger barrier island and wildlife refuge south of Ocean City. It is the home to a herd of the now famous wild ponies. Most of mainland Worcester County consists of quiet picture perfect towns such as Berlin and Snow Hill.

The Eastern Shore is a unique area, much of which remains un-discovered. Whether you visit for the ocean, for the scenery or the history you will find yourself enchanted by the experience.

Turkey Point Lighthouse

Rodgers Tavern, Perryville

CECIL COUNTY

Cecil County is at the very top of the Chesapeake Bay. Geographically it has one "foot" in Central Maryland and the other in the Eastern Shore. In every other aspect it is the Eastern Shore.

TURKEY POINT LIGHT HOUSE - is in Elk Neck State Park. It is situated at the very end of the peninsula and requires a three mile hike to reach it. Both the hike and the view are more than worth the effort. **RODGERS TAVERN** - is a beautifully named and restored 18th century Inn. It was a favorite stopping place for such Colonial fathers as Washington and Jefferson as they traveled back and forth from Washington to Philadelphia.

ELK NECK STATE PARK - is located at the end of a large peninsula jutting out into the top of the Chesapeake Bay. These 150 to 200 foot cliffs are an exception for the Eastern Shore and upper Bay. Probably formed during the ice age, they seem to anchor the top of the Bay. The park affords great hiking, fishing and some of the best scenic views of the bay imaginable.

Chesapeake City

CHESAPEAKE CITY - Located on the C&D Canal, right under the tall bridge, which seems like a
roller coaster - it goes up and down so fast, is Chesapeake City. The town is a study of contrasts.
Part of the town seems "locked" in time, 50 years ago, and the other part is rapidly moving into the present,
full of wonderful old houses, shops, and restaurants.

FOXCATCHER FALLS COVERED BRIDGE - is one of the most hidden covered bridges in the state. It is still in use north of Appleton somewhere in the Fair Hill Natural Resources Area. You need to enter what looks like a farm and follow the road about four miles till you come to this wondrous bridge. There are no signs.

KENT COUNTY

Located just below Cecil County, the entire county is quiet, sophisticated and is a beautiful upper bay area.

CHESTERTOWN - Chestertown is one of the most delightful towns on the Eastern Shore.
Most of the houses range from incredible to unbelievable. Chestertown is one of those places that, once you
have visited, you will need to return.

CHESTERTOWN - It seems as if everyone in the town has their own well trained, full time caretaker. Of course Chestertown is much like the rest of the county and the upper bay. The houses vary greatly in style from this beautiful Victorian manor to some of the finest brick work mansions outside of Annapolis. The Chester River runs through the town and is a source of great seafood and scenic access to the bay.

Washington College, Chestertown

Farm, in Tolchester area

WASHINGTON COLLEGE, CHESTERTOWN - is the first college to be established in the United States.
It was founded in 1782. The campus is as equally beautiful as is everything in Chestertown. Of course
there is a statue of George Washington at the entrance. The farm above is located northeast of Chestertown
and is an example of one of the many farms which reflect the beauty of Kent County.

Rock Hall, Fishing Boats

ROCK HALL - If you don't like fish, you won't like Rock Hall. The town seems to be dedicated to oysters, crabs and fin fish in any size, shape or form. There is a waterman's museum in Rock Hall which is small but delightful museum which of course like everything else in the town is centered upon fish and the men who catch them.

QUEEN ANNE'S COUNTY

Queen Anne's County is located south of the Chester River and Kent County. Much like its neighbor it is split between farms and the water.

KENT ISLAND, BOAT DOCKS - Setting foot on Kent Island from the Bay Bridge, the first thing you become aware of is the water and boats.

THE CHESAPEAKE BAY BRIDGE - The first span of the William Preston Lane Memorial Bridge was completed in 1952. To everyone in Maryland this 4.3 mile long span of the bay is known as the Chesapeake Bay Bridge. A parallel bridge was completed in 1973 to accommodate the growth in traffic which peaks in the summer weekends with travelers to Ocean City.

FARMS OF QUEEN ANNE'S COUNTY - The farms of Queen Anne's County are some of the most productive in the state. With rich soil stretching out over hundreds of flat acres, this land is well suited for farming

Historic Courhouse, Centerville

CENTERVILLE - is in Queen Anne's County. It is rich with numerous historic houses.
THE CENTERVILLE COURTHOUSE - is at one end of the park, in the center of town which is
home to a bronze statue of Queen Anne. The Courthouse is the oldest in Maryland and has been in
continuous use since 1792.

CAROLINE COUNTY

Caroline County is to the east of both Queen Anne's and Talbot Counties. It is the only county on the Eastern Shore which doesn't front on either bay or the ocean.

MARTINAK STATE PARK - Located just out of Denton on the Choptank River this park is renowned for its bass fishing. The scenery and the hiking are equally good.

FARMS, CAROLINE COUNTY - The farms of Caroline County are extremely productive and beautiful at the same time. The soil is rich and flat. The growing season is long and warm.

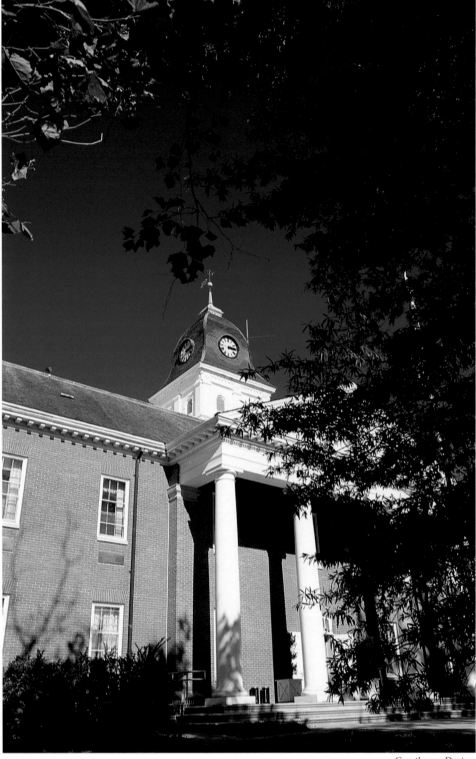

Courthouse, Denton

Historic House, Denton

DENTON - is a rather small town if compared with many cities in Central Maryland. This is where much of its charm lies. It is quiet, peaceful, clean, and friendly. **THE DENTON COURTHOUSE** - is in the square at the center of the town. Surrounding the courthouse are some stunning houses and churches.

TUCKAHOE STATE PARK - is named after the Tuckahoe Creek which flows through the park and is a tributary of the mighty Choptank River. Tuckahoe is a rather large park which affords visitors great fishing, hiking and boating.

TALBOT COUNTY

Talbot County is located south of Queen Anne's County and west of Caroline County. It is laced with rivers, creeks and inlets of all sizes and shapes.

ST. MICHAEL'S - is located out along the twisting and turning thin peninsula past Easton. Above is a view of the Maritime Museum, from the Miles River.

TILGHMAN ISLAND - is located at the very end of the long peninsula on which St. Michael's is located.
Land and water form a symbiotic relationship here. The land is low and it seems like the tide is always high.
Fishing boats and pleasure boats tie up for the evening as the sun begins to set.

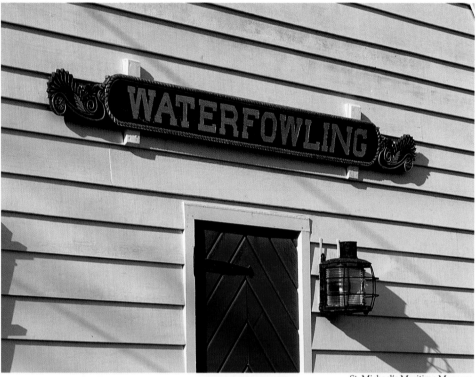

St. Michael's Maritime Museum

St. Michael's Maritime Museum

St. Michael's

Easton, Town Hall

EASTON - At the center of Easton is the town hall located in a fenced-in park. Easton is one of the largest cities on the Eastern Shore. **ST. MICHAEL'S** - once a quiet little town, is now an upscale tourist mecca. **ST. MICHAEL'S MARITIME MUSEUM** - is a huge collection of maritime memorabilia.

St. Michael's Maritime Museum

Black Walnut Point

ST. MICHAEL'S MARITIME MUSEUM - One of the largest collections of maritime antiques, the center of which is the Hooper Strait Lighthouse. Displays are housed in numerous old residences and boat houses. There are restored old skipjacks, log canoes and other boats that can be seen docked at their piers.
BLACK WALNUT POINT - is important only for someone who has visited on a beautiful day when the wind and the waves from the bay are breaking on the shore.

WYE OAK - The Wye Oak is maybe the only site worth seeing off the water in Talbot County. Considering that there is a stream near the Wye Oak like everything else in Talbot it is not that far from the water. This 450 year old tree is the official state tree. It is the largest white oak in the U.S. It began to grow less than 50 years after Columbus supposedly discovered America.

ST. MICHAEL'S LOG CANOE RACES - are held in the summer each year. These restored old sailboats used to be a major source of transportation for the Eastern Shore. Before the Bay Bridge was completed almost everything that came and went from the Eastern Shore did so on the water.

Cambridge, Granmar House

DORCHESTER COUNTY

CAMBRIDGE - Sitting on the south side of the mighty Choptank River, Cambridge is a rather large wonderful old city. It is full of historic houses. The styles of the houses vary from Victorian to Georgian to Colonial. One thing that doesn't vary is the unique beauty of the town. Annie Oakley, the Wild West sharp shooter, is one of the famous people who lived in Cambridge in the early 1900's.

CAMBRIDGE - The town of Cambridge is full of more than historic houses. Setting on the Choptank River it is also full of marinas and boat docks and seafood. The Cambridge City Hall can be seen across this inlet. Further down the creek you can see the fishermen off loading their catches.

Spocott Windmill

Old Boats

Blackwater Area

Skipjack on Small Creek

RURAL DORCHESTER - Much of the rest of Dorchester County is the same way it was a hundred years ago. Pictured above is some of the rural scenes around the **BLACKWATER REFUGE**. Skipjacks pull right up to the door of their owners' house. Old boats in the process of recycling sit on the shore awaiting their fate.
The **SPOCOTT WINDMILL** - is the only existing windmill for grinding wheat in Maryland.

BLACKWATER NATIONAL WILDLIFE REFUGE - is a huge area in the middle of the county. Named after the Blackwater River, this vast marsh land is home to numerous species of wildlife. There are guided tours available but if you just explore this area you will find any number of memorable scenes like the above.

SOMERSET COUNTY

Somerset County sits at the very bottom of the Chesapeake Bay side of the Eastern Shore. Like Talbot and Dorchester it is quiet, rural, and very sophisticated in its own right.

TWIGGS POINT, DEAL ISLAND - is not one of the largest or most visited places in the state but it is truly one of the most picturesque as Skipjacks and fishing boats come and go.

DEAL ISLAND - is another small town with a marina, restaurant, and of course fishing boats.
A sailboat comes in from a day of sailing to tie up in the harbor. Land and water seem to become one
as the sun sets over the Bay.

CRISFIELD - is at the very bottom of the Chesapeake side of the Eastern Shore. If there is a seafood capital of Maryland it would have to be Crisfield. There are fishing boats everywhere you look. Cruises to both Tangier Island and Smith Island leave throughout the day from the center of town.

Teakle Mansion, Princess Anne

PRINCESS ANNE - is one of the largest small towns in Somerset County. It is rich with well kept historic houses and gardens. The best of these is the massive **TEAKLE MANSION** - Built in 1801 by a wealthy merchant, it is like something out of the film "Gone With The Wind".

WICOMICO COUNTY

Wicomico County is wedged between Dorchester County and Somerset County on the west and Worcester County on the east. It is a transition county in the sense that it ties the western bay side with the Ocean side and Worcester County on the east.

NEWTOWN HISTORIC DISTRICT, SALISBURY - Most people "zoom" through Wicomico County in a rush to reach the Ocean. The beauty of the houses in the Newtown area are probably a surprise to anyone who has not explored Salisbury and Wicomico County.

POPLAR HILL MANSION - Located in Salisbury, this 1805 Federal Period Mansion is noted for its exterior details. It is equally refined on the inside. Salisbury is also known for its zoo and park as well as Salisbury State University.

FARM, WICOMICO COUNTY - Much of Wicomico County remains as it was 100 years ago.
The farm shown above reflects one of numerous farms seen throughout the county. The land here is very rich
and favorable for growing most crops.

NANTICOKE - Both the Nanticoke and the Wicomico Rivers run through the county. Actually there are two Wicomico Rivers in Maryland, one is in Wicomico County and the other is between Charles and St. Mary's County in Southern Maryland. In Nanticoke, one of the numerous small towns along the river of the same name you can find beautiful areas and marsh lands which are rich in wildlife.

WORCESTER COUNTY

Worcester County occupies all of the ocean area of the state. The rest of the county is rich in history and scenic beauty, but it is the barrier island along the Atlantic which draws most visitors to the county.

OCEAN CITY - There is little doubt why so many people rush to Ocean City during the summer. It is the beach and the surf. Whether you want a crowded or quiet beach, want to scream around the bay on a jet ski, or watch the bodies on the beach you can find it in Ocean City.

NORTH OCEAN CITY - Above the Route 90 bridge, which was not too long ago a desolate stretch of beach has become home to numerous high rise condominiums. As the sun rises on these buildings across the Assawoman Bay, the residents begin another day of swimming and sun bathing. These condominiums and their residents are responsible for making Ocean City a year round resort.

Golf Course

Berlin

Assateague Island

Boat in the Atlantic Ocean

ASSATEAGUE ISLAND - is a much large barrier island south of Ocean City. Most of it is a large state and federal wildlife preserve. This golf course in **OCEAN PINES** - on the mainland side of the bay is one of numerous courses which have been opened in the last couple of years to accommodate golfers. **BERLIN** - is one of the numerous historic towns on the mainland side of Worcester County.

OCEAN CITY - The Atlantic Ocean is the magnet which brings most people to Worcester County. The waves in the morning relax and renew visitors from throughout the state and region. As crowded as some sections of beach are in lower Ocean City, there are numerous tranquil beaches to the north.

POINT LOOKOUT, ST. MARY'S COUNTY - reflects the magical beauty of Southern Maryland. This is
the most southern point in St. Mary's County. It is hard to believe that this is one of the least known and
visited areas of the state. Southern Maryland is the most historic, in that it was here that the first settlers
landed, its farms are beautiful and its rivers and waters are perfect for fishing and boating.

SOUTHERN MARYLAND

In 1607 Captain John Smith was the first European to explore Southern Maryland and the watershed areas of the Potomac and Patuxent Rivers. He noted in his ship's log that the area was "fruitful and delightsome". Although much has changed in the past 350 years much has remained the same in Southern Maryland.

Southern Maryland is made up of three counties. There is St. Mary's at the south, Calvert on the east, and Charles on the west. Southern Maryland fans out south of Annapolis to form a rather large fingered peninsula. This area is the flood plain and marshes of the hills in Central Maryland and the mountains to the west. The land in Southern Maryland is low, flat, and rich in nutrients and minerals. To the east it is defined by the Chesapeake Bay. To the south and west its' boundary is the wide Potomac River. In places the Potomac River, south of Washington, spans to over five miles across. The peninsula is divided by smaller rivers flowing length wise. Most notably is the Patuxent River in the east and the Wicomico River slightly to the west. Numerous smaller rivers and creeks divide the land as they slowly flow into the Bay.

This area and the lives of it's residents are closely related to the water of it's rivers, creeks and bays. Fishing and crabbing are traditional industries as is farming and agriculture. The number one crop for years in southern Maryland has been tobacco. It has been grown in these counties for over 350 years. Tobacco barns specially designed for storing and drying the leaves are seen throughout the area.

A trip to Southern Maryland though only a short ride from either Annapolis or Washington seems to cover a century of change. The appearance and feeling of much of Southern Maryland is that of a quieter more peaceful era. The hustle and bustle of Washington or Annapolis just doesn't exist and doesn't seem important. Southern Maryland has remained one of the best kept secrets even to most Marylanders.

A short ride south of Annapolis and you are in Calvert County. The county stretches south like a giant finger wedged between the Chesapeake Bay and the Patuxent River. It is ever so slightly higher on the eastern side along the Bay. Most of it's creeks flow west into the Patuxent River. The most dramatic evidence of this elevation can be seen at Calvert Cliffs where the hills of the Cliffs meet the Bay. The erosion from the waves has, over the years, uncovered pre-historic marine fossils. But the mandatory walk to the cliffs through the state park will impress upon you how gently the creeks flow to the bay. In places, these creeks widen to form wetlands a half mile wide. Just outside of Prince Frederick, the County seat, is the Battle Creek Cyprus Swamp. The beaches along the Chesapeake Bay are wide and picturesque. Chesapeake Beach in the north of the county is home to many large marinas and a Railway museum. The largest employer in Calvert County is the Baltimore Gas and Electric Company's nuclear power plant at Calvert Cliffs. Unless you tour it's visitors center or spotted signs leading to it, you would not know the power plant even existed. Solomons Island in the southernmost part of the county is a quiet waterfront community with a deep and well protected harbor. The Calvert Marine Museum is located in Solomons. The center point of the museum is the Drum Point Lighthouse, a "screw pile" lighthouse circa 1883.

Charles County encompasses most of the western part of the Southern Maryland peninsula. It is bordered by Prince George's County to the north, St. Mary's County to the east and the Potomac River forms a semicircle around it to the west. Farming and fishing are it's traditional industries. La Plata is the County seat and is located almost in the very center of the county. Like much of Southern Maryland it is quiet and it's character needs to be slowly uncovered. The largest employer of the county is the Naval Surface Warfare Center at Indian Head. It is located in the northernmost part of the county on a large peninsula jutting into the Potomac River. Indian Head is responsible for developing and testing most of the Navy's high-tech weapon systems. Just south of Indian Head is Smallwood State Park. The centerpiece of this 630 acre recreation area is the restored home of General Smallwood, a Revolutionary War hero. The park, located on the Potomac River, has a large marina, numerous hiking paths and facilities for camping. Further down the Potomac River is the Port Tobacco Courthouse, the remains of what was a thriving port through the Revolutionary War. Dr. Samuel Mudd's house is in the north east part of the county. Dr. Mudd became famous because he set the broken leg of President Lincoln's assassin, John Wilkes Booth. The house and farm have been restored and are open for tours. Some of the most breathtaking points of the county are not listed on the map as historic sites or points of interest, but are down the small country roads leading to wonderful vistas of farms or a panoramic view of the Potomac.

At the very bottom of the Southern Maryland peninsula is St. Mary's County. Leonardtown, the County Seat, is located in the middle. The Naval Surface Warfare Center at the Patuxent River is the largest employer in the county. This is truly an immense Naval base employing over 7,000 people with plans to expand to 12,000 in the next couple of years. The primary mission of the base is the testing and evaluation of Naval aircraft. Adjacent to the airbase, in Lexington Park, is the nation's only museum dedicated to the testing of naval aircraft. The heart of St. Mary's County is St. Mary's City where colonization was established in 1634. An 800 acre outdoor history museum is open to the public in St. Mary's City. There is a working replica of the "Dove", one of the two ships which first brought settlers to Maryland. There is the reconstructed State House of 1676 and the Godiah Spray Tobacco Plantation. There is also Farthings Ordinary, a working replica of a 17th century inn as well as a Native American longhouse. This is truly one of Maryland's historic treasures. Further south is Point Lookout State Park where the Chesapeake Bay and the Potomac River meet. Sotterly Plantation located on the Patuxent River is a completely restored colonial plantation. Other important sites are St. Clement's Island, where the first settlers landed, and the Piney Point Lighthouse.

Southern Maryland is one of the undiscovered treasures of the state. Whether you visit for the scenery, recreation, or the history you will find yourself enlightened by the experience.

Boats in marsh, St. Mary's City

Piney Point Lighthouse

ST MARY'S COUNTY

St. Mary's County is at the very bottom of the Southern Maryland Peninsula. It is the place where the first settlers landed in Maryland on March 25th in 1634.

ST. MARY'S CITY - These boats lyrically remind us of the richness of the two mainstays of this region - the rich farmland and abundance on the water surrounding the land. **PINEY POINT LIGHTHOUSE** - was the first permanent lighthouse built on the Potomac River, (circa 1836).

HISTORIC ST. MARY'S CITY, FARTHINGS ORDINARY - is the re-creation of the original tavern in St. Mary's City. The hosts of historic St. Mary's City are all in period dress, busy doing what they would have been doing in the 1600's, when this town was the center of commerce and trade for Maryland. The hosts of St. Mary's City bring this area alive for visitors and are happy and able to answer almost all historic questions.

Historic St. Mary's City, Farthings Ordinary

Historic St. Mary's City, Military Muster

Historic St. Mary's City, Military Muster

Historic St. Mary's City, Indian Longhouse

HISTORIC ST. MARY'S CITY - has been under restoration for years. On the site of the original town in Maryland, the State of Maryland is rebuilding some of the houses, taverns and farms of this historic area. The original State House has been re-constructed and hosts the military muster each fall. This brings together groups of military regiment from the 1600's. Pikemen and musketeers armed with matchlocks camp and parade about the city. The Indian Longhouse is a re-creation of Indian life in the 1600's.

THE DOVE, HISTORIC ST. MARY'S CITY - The original ships which landed in Maryland from England in 1634 were the "Ark" and the "Dove". A re-creation of the original "Dove" is docked at St. Mary's City. It is still sailed along the St. Mary's River by sailors in original costume. Although the "Dove" does tour about, most of the time you can find it docked in Historic St. Mary's City.

THE NAVAL TEST AND EVALUATION MUSEUM - is just outside the Patuxent River Naval Air Station in Lexington Park. "Pax River" as it is called, is home to The U.S. Naval Test Pilots' School. Astronauts Glenn, Shepperd, Schirra, and Carpenter received test pilot training here. Pax River is the largest employer in St. Mary's County and the base is scheduled for a major expansion in the next couple of years.

SOTTERLEY PLANTATION - is a restored Colonial plantation on the Patuxent River. This magnificent working plantation consists of a farm museum, formal gardens, north and south gatehouses, and outbuildings. The mansion and the grounds are open for tours or group affairs.

CHARLES COUNTY

North and west of St. Mary's County is Charles County. It is bordered on the west by the Potomac River.
It is full of historic monuments, farms and fishing piers.

PORT TOBACCO - The Port Tobacco River flows south from Port Tobacco into the wide Potomac River.
This was a major seaport in the 17th century. Some of the original structures have been restored and are
open for tours.

POTOMAC RIVER - is wide and deep in the portion that flows around Charles County.
The Potomac is perfect for recreational boating and fishing. It is equally great to just watch as the
sun sets and enjoy the beauty.

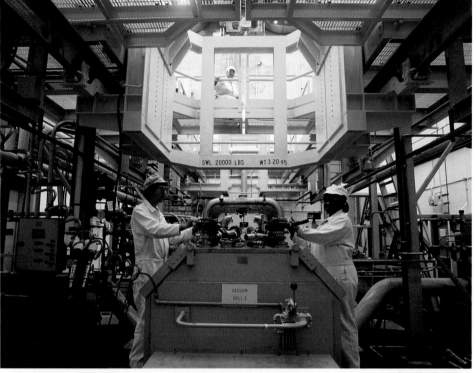

General Smallwood's House

Indian Head - NSWC

Indian Head - NSWC

Dr. Samuel Mudd's House

INDIAN HEAD, NSWC - is a large Naval base in the northwest corner of Charles County. It is responsible for the development and testing of most of the Naval weapon systems. It is the largest employer in the county. **GENERAL SMALLWOOD'S HOUSE** - A Revolutionary War hero, General Smallwood's house has been restored and surrounded by a 630 acre recreational area.
DR. SAMUEL MUDD'S HOUSE - The house and farm belonging to the doctor who set John Wilkes Booth's leg, is now restored and is open for tours.

AMISH FARMER - The Amish farmer reflects Charles County's rich agricultural tradition. The quiet rustic charm of Charles County can be seen and felt when traveling down just about any of the small roads. This is much the way it was a hundred years ago.

CALVERT COUNTY

Calvert County is a long slender county, at the top of the eastern side of the Southern Maryland Peninsula. The County is noted for its farms, fishing and historic sites.

CALVERT MARINE MUSEUM - is at the southernmost point of Calvert County on Solomons Island. The Drum Point Lighthouse, a "screw-pile" lighthouse, is at the center of an extensive maritime collection.

SOLOMONS ISLAND - A protected harbor and the small town of Solomons Island at the end of Calvert County reflects the maritime tradition of the county. This is the perfect location to fish either the Chesapeake Bay or the Patuxent or Potomac Rivers. It is also the perfect place to relax and enjoy the numerous sites or eat in some of the local restaurants.

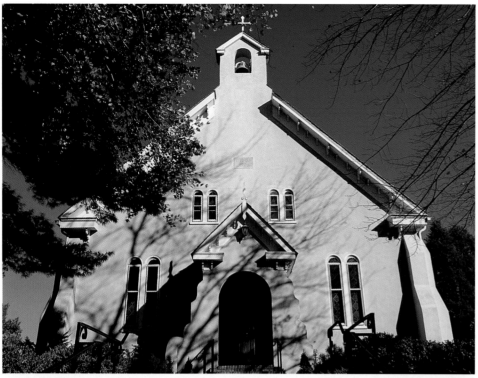
All Saints Episcopal Church

Tobacco Barn

Battle Creek Cyprus Swamp

Railway Museum, Chesapeake City

BATTLE CREEK CYPRUS SWAMP - is a 100 acre sanctuary which is home to the northernmost cyprus swamp in North America. **ALL SAINTS EPISCOPAL CHURCH** - circa 1692, is one of the numerous historic churches in Calvert County. **RAILWAY MUSEUM IN CHESAPEAKE CITY** - is a small but nice museum housed in a 1898 railway station. Chesapeake Beach, the town surrounding the museum, is full of great beaches and marinas.

CALVERT CLIFFS - is probably the best known site to visit in Calvert County. It is a large recreational area with nature walks, woods, marshland, and the cliffs rich in archeological treasures.

Mountains, Garrett County

GARRETT COUNTY MOUNTAINS - Each area of Maryland has its own unique character. Nothing reflects the beauty and uniqueness of Western Maryland better than the mountains and deep valleys of this region. In the past it would take weeks of travel on horseback to reach these mountains. Today you can reach the mountains in a few hours.

WESTERN MARYLAND

Western Maryland includes five counties to the west of the urban areas of Central Maryland. Western Maryland is full of mountains, valleys and waterfalls. It is as if it were a completely different state compared to the wetlands of the Eastern Shore or Southern Maryland or the cosmopolitan areas of Central Maryland. Western Maryland is not far removed from either Baltimore or Washington. It is not even that far from St. Mary's City or Salisbury. It is amazing how many Marylanders think it is a long trip and have never explored the area. Those that have, fall in love at first mountain and, find themselves returning again and again.

Western Maryland in a real sense is the source of wealth and richness for the state. If it were not for the mountains and dense forests of this region the fields in Central, Southern, and the Eastern Shore would not be rich in minerals and nutrients. The mountains are the "well spring" of most of the rivers which flow through Maryland. The mountains are also protection for the fields and towns to the east. They are a natural barrier for the harsh winds of the north and central plains.

The last area to be settled, Western Maryland can be measured as much by it's mountains as the independent spirit of it's residents. This is the result of the hardy nature of the settlers which made Western Maryland their home. Beside the obvious challenges of distance and mountains, the growing season is shorter in Western Maryland.

Carroll County is a transition county. It is in a sense a "bedroom" area for both Baltimore and Washington, but few of the urban influences are present. The hills in Carroll County begin to roll a little higher than they do to the east. At the same time it is the attitude of the residents which makes it more a part of Western Maryland. Westminster is quiet and much the way it was a century ago. The town is perfectly happy to have the Carroll County Farm Museum almost in the center of town. Most important of all the residents don't look to Baltimore or Washington for much of anything but an occasional visit to a museum or the symphony. Uniontown to the west of Westminster is a perfect example of small-town life a hundred years ago. Much of the beauty in Carroll County lies in the area between towns. Well kept farms are situated between forests, hills, and streams. There is an elegant balance here, such as in Taneytown in the northwest part of the county. Surrounded by farms and cows, it is also home to Antrim 1844. This inn is a perfect example of the county's rustic elegance.

Frederick County, to the west of Carroll County is where the mountains begin. From the hill in Mount Airy along I-70 just across the border you can see the ridge of mountains stretching north and south 20 miles beyond. The city of Frederick is a model city at the foot of these mountains. Most of the shops and houses have been perfectly restored. To the north of Frederick along the ridge of the mountains is Catoctin Mountain National Park. Camp David, the president's country retreat, is located here. Cunningham Falls State Park just next door is home of a picturesque waterfalls. The Grotto of Lourdes and the Mother Seton Shrine are north of both parks. Just east of the Catoctin Mountains along some of the streams and tributaries of the Monocacy River are three covered bridges built in the 1850's.

As you cross the second ridge of mountains, west of Frederick you enter Washington County. By the 1730's these mountain passes had been breached and settlers were establishing farms in the valleys. Among the first was Jonathan Hager. In 1739 his house "Hager's Fancy" was built in what would become Hagerstown. This is now the largest city in Washington County. In the 1750's British and American troops used Hagerstown and Ft. Frederick, to the west, as staging areas in the French and Indian War. Ft. Frederick has been restored and through most of the spring, summer and fall you can watch reenactments of life in the 1750's. The first monument to honor George Washington is of course in Washington County. Not far from the Washington Monument are the Crystal Grottoes Caverns, the only caves open for tours in Maryland. Antietam National Battlefield is located just outside of Sharpsburg. Washington County is home to more 19th century stone bridges than any other region of the country. Sidling Hill, to the west has an exhibition center where you can view Interstate 68 as it passes through this man made cut in the mountain.

Allegany County begins just beyond Sidling Hill, and is one of the two counties in Maryland whose names have their roots in the Native Indian language. Allegany means "beautiful stream" and, this is exactly what visitors have found for the last two hundred and fifty years. The mountains do not peak much higher here, they are just more numerous. The valleys are deeper, the farms are fewer, and the forests are more plentiful. Green Ridge State Park seems to occupy the entire eastern part of the county. The C&O Canal and the Potomac run along the bottom of the county. Cumberland is the largest city in Allegany County. It is situated in a valley surrounded by mountains. This used to be the crossroad of the National road, the C&O Canal, and the B&O Railroad. Most of these are long since gone but the railroad has been reborn. The Western Maryland Scenic Railroad now runs through Cumberland. There is a railroad museum, quaint shops and hundreds of happy passengers can be found when the old steam engine puffs into the station. In LaValle, just west of Cumberland on Route 40, is The Old Toll Gate House from the original National Road. Frostburg is the home to Frostburg State College and just beyond lies Garrett County.

Garrett County corners the market for the largest, highest, newest, and yes the coldest. Deep Creek Lake is the largest fresh water lake in Maryland. Backbone Mountain is the highest at 3,360 feet above sea level. Wisp is the state's largest ski area and Garrett County is the newest county in Maryland at just over a century old. Deep Creek Lake is the county's recreational focal point. A man made lake, it was created in 1925 by the completion of the Deep Creek Dam. Visitors enjoy boating of every kind in the summer. There is fishing for walleye, yellow perch, and pike. There are two stunning waterfalls close by in Swallow Falls State Park. The Youghiogheny River flows through the western part of the county and the Savage River flows through the eastern part. Both rivers are a source of canoeing, rafting, fishing, and camping.

The mountains and lakes of Western Maryland are one of the natural treasures of our state. Whether you visit for the scenery, recreation or the history you will find yourself enchanted.

Western Maryland College, Westminster

New Windsor Farm

CARROLL COUNTY

Located just west of Baltimore County, Carroll County is the beginning of Western Maryland. The environment is more rural than urban in Carroll County.

WESTERN MARYLAND COLLEGE - is located in Westminster, the county seat. It is a 4 year independent college with 1200 undergraduates and approximately 1000 graduate students. **NEW WINDSOR** - is a bit south of Uniontown and echoes the agricultural charm of Carroll County. The rolling hills of the county are full of picturesque farms at every turn.

FARM, UNIONTOWN AREA - Carroll County has experienced much growth in the last 10 years.
Although it has become a "bedroom" community for both the urbanites of Baltimore and Washington,
most of the county is still full of beautiful working farms. A friendly rustic independence marks the spirit
of Carroll County residents.

Carroll County Farm Museum

Carroll County Farm Museum

Carroll County Farm Museum - Lambs

CARROLL COUNTY FARM MUSEUM - The Carroll County Farm Museum is located almost in the heart of Westminster. It portrays an 1800's farm with a farmhouse, general store, farm equipment, and working demonstrations. The museum is on a 140 acre complex and gives a glimpse of what life in 1852 was like.

Antrim 1844, Drawing Room

Antrim 1844, Clabaugh Room

Antrim 1844, Pool and Gardens

Antrim 1844, Cocktail Party in Dining Room

ANTRIM 1844 - This country inn, resort and restaurant is located in an Antebellum mansion masterfully restored by Dort and Richard Mollett, owners and innkeepers. The numerous rooms are decorated in the elegant decor of fine antiques, fireplaces, canopy beds, and marble baths or jacuzzis. Enjoy the Old World opulence amidst the fine dining and meeting rooms, tennis courts, swimming pool, croquet lawn and putting green nestled in the Carroll County countryside. Antrim 1844 offers the idyllic setting for a romantic weekend, memorable wedding retreat, or productive corporate meeting.

125

Roddy Road Covered Bridge

Utica Mills Covered Bridge

Roddy Road Covered Bridge

FREDERICK COUNTY

Just west of Carroll County is Frederick County. Here is where the mountains of Western Maryland begin in earnest.

RODDY ROAD COVERED BRIDGE - is one of the three beautiful 1850-60's covered bridges in Frederick County.
UTICA MILLS COVERED BRIDGE - is also located in the picturesque area of Thurmont in the northern part of the county. These bridges were built with covers to protect them from weathering.

AERIAL VIEW OF FREDERICK COUNTY - Taken just east of the town of Frederick, this view looking northwest captures some of the beauty of the entire county. In the distance the blue mountains can be seen stretching along the entire horizon from north to south.

Frederick, Christmas House Tour

Cunningham Falls, Thurmont

FREDERICK - The town of Frederick is one of the most beautiful in Maryland. At the foot of the Catoctin Mountains, it is brimming with old homes that have been meticulously restored, antique shops and restaurants. Each Christmas, numerous houses are open for a house tour.

CUNNINGHAM FALLS - Located just north of Frederick near Thurmont is the Cunningham Falls State Park. The falls is a 78 foot high waterfall that runs through a rocky gorge.

Hunting Creek Lake

CUNNINGHAM FALLS STATE PARK - is just south of the Catoctin State Park. The falls and the Little Hunting Creek are full of amazingly beautiful forests and vistas. **HUNTING CREEK LAKE** - is located in the Cunningham Falls State Park and offers a quiet place for fishing and boating.

Stone Bridges, Hagerstown

WASHINGTON COUNTY

Washington County begins just as you descend the mountains west of Frederick. The mountains don't get that much higher, there are just more of them in Washington County.

STONE BRIDGES - both north and south of Hagerstown, along the Antietam River, you will find in Washington County some of the finest stone bridges ever constructed circa 1800's. Most of these bridges were built as part of the first National Road or to develop transportation routes to the road.

SIDLING HILL SCENIC - The countryside of Washington County is some of the nicest land in the state. The farms in these valleys grow crops in rich soil. Farmers here need to plow their land and plant their crops carefully because they have a shorter growing season than the farms in Central Maryland and the Eastern Shore.

Washington Monument

Crystal Grottoes Caverns

Ft. Frederick

CRYSTAL GROTTOES CAVERNS - are the only underground caves open to the public in Maryland. **WASHINGTON MONUMENT** - is the first monument dedicated to Washington in the country. It was built by the residents of Boonsboro in 1827. **FT. FREDERICK** - is a fort originating from the French and Indian War located outside of Big Pool. It has been carefully restored and throughout the year hosts demonstrations of life as it was in the early 1700's.

TOUR DU PONT, HAGERSTOWN - Historic Hagerstown becomes a bit "racy" as the Tour Du Pont finishes a leg of the race in this quiet town. Filled with historic sites, restored houses and restaurants, Hagerstown is a perfect stopping point on a drive through Western Maryland.

133

ANTIETAM OVERLOOK FARM B&B - Antietam Overlook Farm is a quiet, secluded mountaintop country inn. It is perched on a high elevation, giving guests a spectacular view overlooking Antietam National Battlefield and the historic village of Sharpsburg, Maryland. Harpers Ferry and Shepherdstown, West Virginia are just minutes away.

ILLUMINATION AT ANTIETAM NATIONAL BATTLEFIELD - The Battle of Antietam, just outside of Sharpsburg, was the most devastating single day of fighting in the Civil War. Each December volunteers light 23,111 candles to honor those who lost their life fighting for our country on that day of battle. Civil War re-enactments also take place during the illumination.

135

Allegany County - Autumn Foliage

ALLEGANY COUNTY

Named by a native indian word meaning "beautiful stream", Allegany County is sandwiched between Washington County and Garrett County in Western Maryland.

GREEN RIDGE STATE FOREST - The mountain terrain is destined for all to enjoy in Green Ridge State Forest. Touching three different mountains and running along the Potomac River, it covers almost one third of eastern Allegany County.

CUMBERLAND - Once the commercial hub of Western Maryland, Cumberland was the cross roads of the C&O Canal, the B&O Railroad, and the original National Road. Today Cumberland is still the center of much heavy and light manufacturing. Due to its numerous historical sites and natural wonders it has also become a center of newly developing tourism.

La Vale Toll Gate House

Western Maryland Scenic Railroad

Western Maryland Scenic Railroad

LA VALE TOLL GATE HOUSE - La Vale Toll Gate House was the only house in Maryland that collected fees from travelers on the Old National Road, the first federally funded highway in the United States.
WESTERN MARYLAND SCENIC RAILROAD - This 1916 Baldwin Steam locomotive runs seasonally taking passengers from Cumberland to Frostburg and back. It is a scenic three hour round trip for anyone who wants to view Western Maryland in a historical and leisurely way.

MOUNT SAVAGE - Mount Savage and the vistas at the western part of Allegany County are breathtaking. This vista was a sunrise over the valleys and mountains outside of Frostburg.

GARRETT COUNTY

The westernmost county in the state, this is also the youngest county in the state at only a little over 100 years old.

MOUNTAINS OF GARRETT COUNTY - are the highest in the state and the valleys are the deepest. They are also some of the most beautiful in Maryland. These mountains are just outside of Deep Creek Lake going south toward Oakland. At the very southern end of Garrett County is the highest mountain in the state, Backbone Mountain, at 3360 feet in elevation.

SWALLOW FALLS STATE PARK - is one of the most amazingly beautiful areas of the state. There are two water falls found in the park. Swallow Falls is the smallest and Muddy Creek Falls is the tallest. The forests surrounding the falls contain many hiking trails and picnic areas.

Forest, Swallow Falls State Park

Road with Fall Foliage

Deep Creek Lake

Muddy Creek Falls

DEEP CREEK LAKE - is a man-made lake in the center of the county. It holds 65 miles of shore line and is the largest fresh water lake in Maryland. Traveling almost any small road around the lake, you will find surprisingly beautiful scenery. **MUDDY CREEK FALLS** - During the winter months, when the weather is cold enough, the falls becomes a monolith of frozen motion.

MUDDY CREEK FALLS - just outside of Deep Creek in Swallow Falls State Park is Muddy Creek Falls.
You can walk beneath the 52 foot waterfall in the summertime if you don't mind getting a little wet.

143

HARLEY FARM B&B - One of Maryland's best kept secrets, Harley Farm Bed & Breakfast (888-231-FARM) is located in the mountains of Western Maryland. Only minutes from Deep Creek Lake and Wisp Ski Resort, the 65 acre farm boasts orchards, wildflower meadows, cornfields, horses, ducks and geese. The owners, Wayne and Kam Gillespie, have decorated the B&B beautifully with collections from their world travels. It's an ideal place for a romantic B&B getaway or a retreat (kgillespie@miworld.net) with workshops in leadership, yoga, health, and art.

WISP SKI RESORT - In McHenry on Deep Creek Lake is the year round ski area and golf resort. Wisp overlooks Deep Creek Lake and the view from the slopes is breathtaking. Besides the accommodations at the ski resort there are numerous lodges, B&B's and restaurants in that area.

THE PORT OF BALTIMORE - Some of the world's largest freighters and container ships travel into the harbor to be loaded and unloaded at the Dundalk and Seagirt Marine Terminals. From its beginnings, Baltimore has been one of the nation's major ports, due to the city's ideal location and its sophisticated railway systems. Since the mid-1950's, with the creation of the Maryland Port Authority (currently the Maryland Port Administration), the state has coordinated efforts to remain on the industry's cutting edge with marine facility developments that are capable of handling cargo from all markets of the world.

146

MARYLAND'S ECONOMY

Over three centuries ago the Maryland economy, much like that of her sister colonies, was tied to soil and water. The vast network of rivers which made their way to the Chesapeake Bay were a major source of food and trade routes. A favorable climate and the rich farm lands of the Eastern Shore, Southern and Central Maryland made it the perfect location to establish prosperous farms. Though isolated at the beginning from the other English settlements, Maryland's location would prove to be auspicious. Philadelphia was a dusty rigorous two-day ride and Washington was over a century in the future. The richness of the land, resourcefulness of her settlers, religious and social tolerance, and the location of Maryland proved economically bountiful from the beginning.

Maryland's economy today in a sense does not bear any resemblance with her early roots. Today the Maryland economy is grounded in high technology, services, international trade, construction and a constantly changing manufacturing base. Professional and technical workers make up over a fifth of the state work force, the highest percentage of any state in the nation.

As much as Maryland has changed she has also remained much the same. Thousands of Marylanders still turn to both the water and the land for their livelihood. Generation after generation of watermen have set their small wooden boats in the waters of the Chesapeake Bay to fish for it's bountiful harvest of crabs, oysters, clams, and fish. There are others who now accommodate the ever increasing pleasure boating industry. Farms throughout Maryland are still a source of bountiful crops, some of which have been owned and operated by the same families for numerous generations. The fields and farms of Maryland are also home to a vast horse breeding and racing industry. The home of the Preakness, Maryland horse breeders raise horses which are world renowned. Tobacco is still king in many respects in the fields of Southern Maryland. Farms on the Eastern Shore and Central Maryland grow wheat, truck produce and delicious corn. The Eastern Shore farms are also a source of a major poultry industry.

Maryland's land and water are in a sense still the backbone of the economy. This is not only in what they produce but also in that it is the land, water, and location that attract new business to the state.

Located in the middle of the busy Atlanta-Boston corridor, Baltimore is a major hub of commercial transportation. The birthplace of modern railroads, Maryland is serviced by both Conrail and the CSX corporation. Both freight and passenger rail service to the state, the eastern seaboard and the nation is excellent. The interstate highway systems slice the state north-to-south and east-to-west permanently linking Maryland with her immediate neighbors and the nation. The Port of Baltimore has, since the founding of the country, been an important center of trade. It has over 45 miles of renewed waterfront and can handle over 200 ships at a time. High speed computerized cranes handle containers and cargo and expedite its transfer to either rail or truck transportation routes. Three major airports serve Maryland residents and visitors.

Baltimore/Washington International Airport has just undergone a major expansion. BWI has added new runways, new passenger facilities, new cargo facilities and an international terminal to better service the area. Maryland is the nation's fourth largest air travel market.

Maryland's location, next to Washington, has been the reason for the development of the I-270 high technology corridor in Montgomery County. There are almost more "national institutes" of almost every type in the corridor than there are in Washington. It is home to the National Medical Library, Bethesda Naval Medical Center and The National Institute of Standards and Technology. There are also hundreds of national associations and businesses which serve the government located in the I-270 corridor. In Prince George's County the influence of Washington can be seen in Andrews Air Force Base. It is the home to Air Force One and the "welcome mat" for the nation. The NASA Goddard Space Flight Center in Prince George's County is responsible for tracking all of our satellites and the development of all our new satellites. In quiet Charles County there is the massive Naval Surface Warfare Center at Indian Head. It employs more PHD's and high technology engineers than some countries have.

All of these influences add up to the general prosperity for Marylanders. The average household income is 10% higher than the national average and unemployment is usually two points below the national average. Certain employment patterns are rapidly changing. Manufacturing jobs are in decline in many sections of the economy, especially in heavy industry. The coal industry of Western Maryland employs only a fraction of the work force it did fifty years ago. The canning industry on the Eastern Shore has declined in the last couple of decades. This has been balanced by the boom in the service sectors, especially in tourist related businesses. In Baltimore, Western Maryland and the Washington Suburbs, tourism has provided numerous jobs that didn't exist ten years ago. The development of high technology industries has produced major opportunities in the last decade. Of the ten largest state employers, six are involved with some aspect of high technology work.

Maryland's adaptability to the changing economic environment has not come without cooperation between the private sector and the state government. Maryland's financial assistance programs have helped new businesses get off the ground and aid the expansion of existing businesses. Maryland has been a leader in establishing enterprise zones that offer various incentives and tax benefits to businesses which choose to move into the state. With the three foreign trade zones, the climate for business is consistently improving.

All of these reasons are important to why so many businesses have decided to make Maryland their home. Maryland also offers diverse housing opportunities, a good climate, an existing network of fine educational and cultural institutions and it is in close proximity to Washington, Philadelphia, and New York. Maryland has much to offer its resident business.

SEAGIRT MARINE TERMINAL - Nearly ten years in the making, the Seagirt Marine Terminal has projected the port of Baltimore into the twenty-first century. The huge, blue twenty-story cranes seem to scrape the sky as they effortlessly unload container cargo ships at record speeds. Opened in late 1989, the $220 million, state-of-the-art terminal can accommodate the largest container ships from around the world. The project, run by Maryland Port Administration, has provided hundreds of jobs for Marylanders, and promises to keep the port on the cutting edge of the marine shipping industry for decades to come.

BALTIMORE-WASHINGTON INTERNATIONAL AIRPORT - The ultra modern design of Baltimore-Washington International Airport practically beckons adventurous globe-trotters to explore far-away lands. Easily accessed and just minutes south of the city, BWI has increased its services to include a multitude of domestic and international airlines and routes, as well as offering an efficient air freight business. Despite its size, the design of the airport gives travelers stress-free access, whether they are entering or leaving the area.

Union Square, Baltimore, Maryland

MARYLAND FILM OFFICE - Behind the scenes, filming in one of the delightful period neighborhoods of Maryland. The Maryland Film Office promotes the state of Maryland's tremendous diversity for location filming by major feature film and television producers. The economic impact of this business exceeds $50 million annually and is expected to approach $100 million in the near future.

Signet Bank Tower

SIGNET BANK - Signet Banking Corporation (http://www.signet.com) is a $12 billion financial institution headquartered in Richmond, Virginia. The company offers a wide array of financial services through its Capital Markets, Commercial and Consumer banking businesses. Signet has offices in Virginia, Maryland and the District of Columbia, and it markets several of its products nationally.

MCI - "Founded in 1968, MCI began as a provider of microwave transmission for commercial trucking companies in the midwest. In 1984, MCI single-handedly took on AT&T and the federal government in the divestiture of long distance telephone service. MCI's Baltimore/Washington Sales Center is an important part of the world's fastest growing, diversified telecommunications company. It offers long distance, local access, paging, wireless, Internet and business software, outsourcing, advanced global telecommunications, and music merchandising."

Electron Beam Lithography Laboratory

NORTHROP GRUMMAN - Northrop Grumman's Electronic Sensors and Systems Division, a defense electronics business based in Linthicum, is Maryland's largest manufacturing employer. The company stays at the forefront of this industry by investing in modern technology such as this Electron Beam Lithography Laboratory. Here operators transfer complex microchip designs onto glass "masks" which are used as stencils to print onto semiconducting materials such as silicon and gallium arsenide. This process produces specialized microchips used on radar systems for the U.S. Army's Longbow Apache helicopter, the U.S. Air Force's F-22 aircraft, and on the Federal Aviation Administration's air traffic control radars.

153

Installation of New Gas Lines

BGE - A large reel that automatically feeds flexible plastic pipe into trenches is making the Baltimore Gas and Electric's natural gas expansion work simpler. The first gas company in the United States, BGE has been extending gas mains to many Central Maryland neighborhoods. Because gas is clean, reliable and cost efficient, the demand for natural gas to heat, cool and fuel homes and businesses has grown dramatically the past several years.

Electric Lines Repair, Baltimore County

BGE - The Baltimore Gas & Electric Company has powered the Baltimore area for nearly
180 years. With more than 17,000 miles of distribution lines, BGE provides electricity to more than
1 million residential and business customers in Baltimore City and it's surrounding counties. Efforts
to continuously upgrade the systems that carry electricity have greatly enhanced BGE's electric reliability
and service to customers.

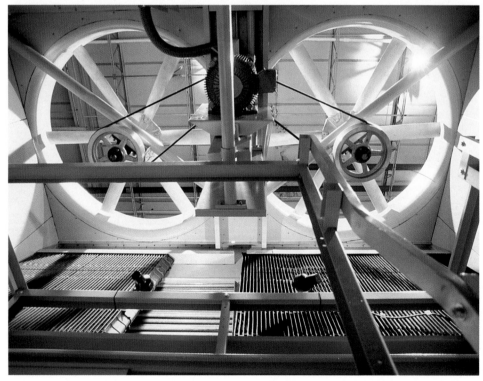

BALTIMORE AIRCOIL COMPANY (BAC) - was founded in 1938 by **John Engalitcheff, Jr.**, and initially manufactured coils for the refrigeration industry. It later expanded into evaporative cooling equipment to serve the refrigeration, industrial process, and the new and developing air-conditioning industries. Today, Baltimore Aircoil is a worldwide manufacturer of evaporative heat transfer and ice thermal storage products and systems which cool and conserve water, conserve energy and reduce global warming. With operations and plants in the U.S., Canada, and other countries throughout the world, its products and services are both domestically and internationally recognized for technological innovation and industry leadership.

Series 1000 Marine Satellite Phone

Network Operations Center, American Mobile Satellite Corp.

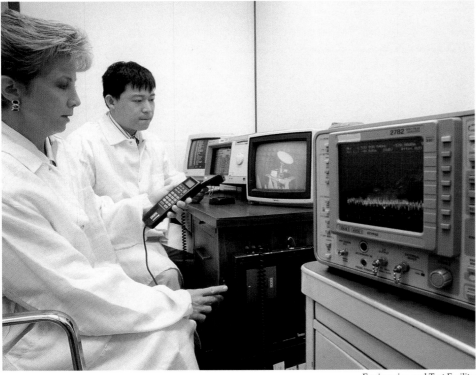

Engineering and Test Facility

Anechoic Chamber

WESTINGHOUSE - Westinghouse builds the Series 1000 Satellite Telephone System. This system allows its user to communicate to or from anywhere in the world, from within the coverage area of a communications satellite. The phone can be used throughout North America, including hundreds of miles off shore. With the Series 1000, digital voice, data or fax calls are made directly to the satellite, 22,000 miles in space, then beamed to the Network Operations Center for distribution over public telephone systems. The phone is available in land mobile, marine, fixed-site, and aeronautical models, and was developed at the Westinghouse Wireless facility in Linthicum. Its antennas underwent testing in a special anechoic chamber monitored by engineers.

Redland Genstar - Texas, Maryland Quarry

Allegheny Power - Dispatch Center

Redland Genstar - Texas, Maryland Quarry

Allegheny Power - Business Location Center

REDLAND GENSTAR - Headquartered in Hunt Valley, Redland Genstar is one of the major Mid-Atlantic suppliers of crushed stone, concrete, blacktop and other construction materials and services. Redland Genstar has been leading this industry for 150 years.
ALLEGHENY POWER - Hagerstown, Maryland-based Allegheny Power supplies electricity to 1.4 million customers in Maryland, Ohio, Pennsylvania, Virginia and West Virginia. Allegheny's sophisticated business center also provides detailed information to business prospects and is helping the Fortune 500 company expand its five-state service territory.

Advanced Manufacturing

Air Traffic Control Systems

Tactical Information Systems

Information Security Systems

ALLIEDSIGNAL - AlliedSignal Aerospace Communications Systems has been headquartered in Towson for more than half a century. The company is a leader in developing, producing and supporting sophisticated combat identification systems, tactical information systems, information security systems and air traffic control systems. AlliedSignal's customers include the U.S. and allied defense, civil aviation and other government agencies. Its advanced manufacturing operations is a high performing center of excellence for AlliedSignal.

159

Frederick, Maryland Plant

Plant #1 Cambridge, Maryland

Plant #2 Cambridge, Maryland

PHILIPS TECHNOLOGIES - a division of Philips Electronics North America Corp., is headquartered in Frederick, MD., and is comprised of two business units. The Airpax Protector Group, with operations in Cambridge and Frederick, MD, Matamoros, Mexico, and Japan, produces circuit breakers, thermostats, and microcircuit packages. The Airpax Mechatronics Group, with operations in Cheshire, CT, Singapore, Malaysia, and Camberly, U.K., produces precision motors. The company serves telecommunications, information processing, office automation, heavy vehicle, and industrial customers worldwide, with highly reliable components engineered and manufactured to the highest standards of quality and customer satisfaction.

Sparks, Maryland, Headquarters

Reagent Filling Operation

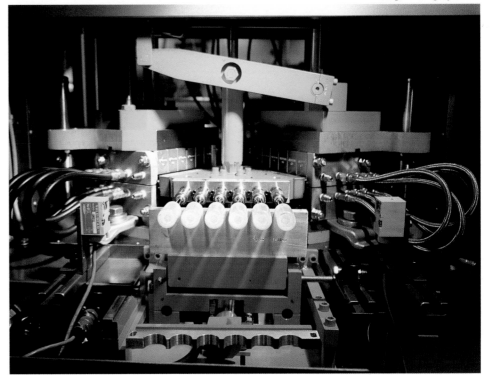

Test Kit Assembly / Quality Control

Injection Blow Molding of Bottles

TAYLOR TECHNOLOGIES - Founded in 1930, Taylor Technologies manufactures products for water analysis in its 60,000-square-foot facility in Sparks, Maryland. The reagents and testing apparatus are used by water analysts worldwide in a variety of applications, including municipal water and wastewater treatment, operational control and regulatory compliance by industry, boiler and cooling water monitoring, aquaculture, and swimming pool / spa testing. Taylor is ranked one of the area's fastest growing technology firms, and its president was named top manufacturing entrepreneur in the state in 1995.

161

THOMPSON STEEL - Thompson Steel Co, Inc, located in Sparrows Point, Maryland is a producer of cold rolled strip steel. Thompson purchases steel coils from suppliers such as nearby Bethlehem Steel, reduces the thickness by cold rolling, heat treats the steel to change it's properties and slits it into narrow strips. The narrow coils are shipped to customers who stamp out a wide variety of products such as bearings, saw blades, hinges and various automotive components.

ENVIRONMENTAL ELEMENTS - Environmental Elements Corporation, with headquarters and research facilities in the Baltimore metropolitan area, provides air pollution management solutions, systems, equipment, and services to customers worldwide. In business more than fifty years, Environmental Elements is the Nation's largest particulate air pollution control equipment supplier to the pulp and paper and the power industries. As gaseous air pollution management received increased attention, Environmental Elements broadened its technological base and introduced unique solutions to gaseous air pollution problems. Long an innovator in air pollution management equipment, Environmental Elements is dedicated to continued technical leadership and to extraordinary customer satisfaction.

163

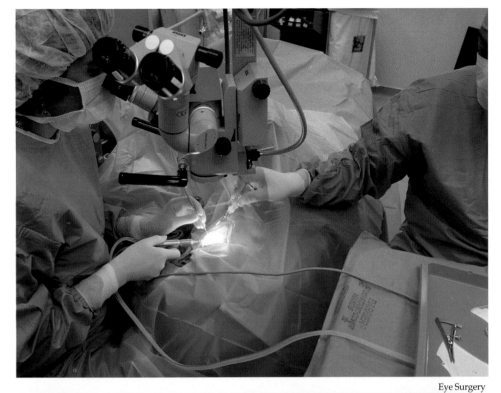

Eye Surgery

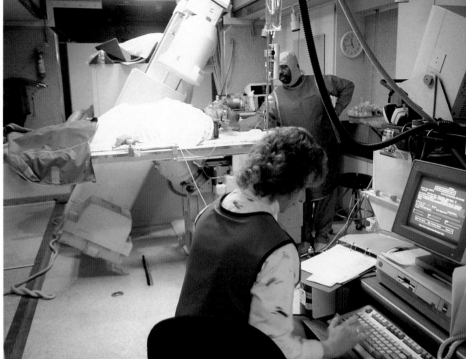

Lithotripsy Procedure Area

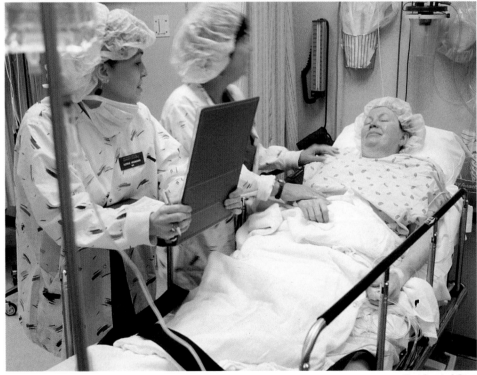

Post Surgical Care

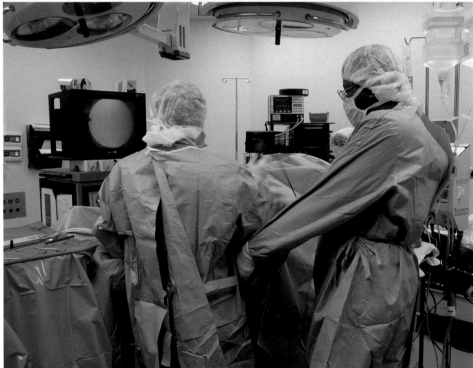

Knee Surgery

HEALTHSOUTH - Central Maryland Surgery Center opened in 1990 as a member of "the Healthcare Company for the 21st Century". On the cutting edge of modern surgery, this freestanding, multi-specialty, outpatient facility provides personalized quality care to Maryland citizens. Furthermore, this setting offers patients, physicians, and the insurance industry flexible scheduling, a more cost-effective alternative to performing surgery, and a network of rehabilitative centers. Experienced professionals, using state of the art equipment, interact warmly with both patient and family members while performing as a unified team. Striving to achieve excellence, HEALTHSOUTH Central Surgery Center is Medicare and JCAHO accredited with commendation.

Solarex

Solarex

Shimadzu

SOLAREX - The Solarex manufacturing facility with its distinctive blue-sloped roof, provides a striking complement to the steepled "skyline" of Frederick. Seen from Interstate 70, it raises lots of eyebrows and invokes many questions. Solarex, the nation's largest US owned producer of solar electric modules, produces a portion of its power requirements from its roof mounted array.

SHIMADZU SCIENTIFIC INSTRUMENTS (SSI) - is one of the three largest analytical instrument manufacturers in the world. Manufacturing in Columbia, Maryland since 1975, SSI is the North and South American subsidiary of Shimadzu Corporation of Japan, a 1.6 billion dollar enterprise with 120 years of expertise.

SCHEER PARTNERS - Scheer Partners is a full service commercial real estate firm specializing in the needs of the Maryland business community. Since it's inception in 1992, Scheer Partners has emerged as the top producer in the Maryland marketplace. The reason for Scheer Partners' success is an unrelenting commitment to the needs of its clients and highly developed specialization in areas such as biotechnology/health science and information technology. Scheer Partners offers a full compliment of real estate services to its clients, including office leasing, land development, investment acquisition and property management.

AT&T - AT&T Submarine Systems, Inc. has its east coast depot in Baltimore, where both the *CS Global Link* and the *CS Global Mariner* are stationed. It is fully staffed on a 24-hour alert to service undersea cable systems in the Atlantic. The Global Link represents the state-of-the-art in cable ship design. Large and powerful, the ship can carry more than 6,000 metric tons of fiber-optic cable. It is maneuverable enough to lower a 2.1 cm cable to within meters of a target 6,000 meters below the ocean. The *C.S. Global Mariner*, the newest addition to the AT&T fleet, can travel 10,000 nautical miles at a peak speed of 13.8 knots without refueling.

DORCHESTER COUNTY SUNSET- Much of southern Dorchester County is quiet and rural.
Down almost any road is water, wetlands, boats or a boat dock. This sunset is looking out at the Honga
River as it flows south to the bay.